Impact Measurement and Outcomes Evaluation Using Salesforce for Nonprofits

A Guide to Data-Driven Frameworks

Dustin MacDonald

Apress®

Impact Measurement and Outcomes Evaluation Using Salesforce for Nonprofits: A Guide to Data-Driven Frameworks

Dustin MacDonald
Sigourney, IA, USA

ISBN-13 (pbk): 978-1-4842-9707-0   ISBN-13 (electronic): 978-1-4842-9708-7
https://doi.org/10.1007/978-1-4842-9708-7

Managing Director, Apress Media LLC: Welmoed Spahr
Acquisitions Editor: Susan McDermott
Development Editor: Laura Berendson
Editorial Project Manager: Gryffin Winkler

Cover designed by eStudioCalamar

Cover image by Mint_Foto from Pixabay

Distributed to the book trade worldwide by Springer Science+Business Media New York, 1 New York Plaza, Suite 4600, New York, NY 10004-1562, USA. Phone 1-800-SPRINGER, fax (201) 348-4505, e-mail orders-ny@ springer-sbm.com, or visit www.springeronline.com. Apress Media, LLC is a California LLC and the sole member (owner) is Springer Science + Business Media Finance Inc (SSBM Finance Inc). SSBM Finance Inc is a **Delaware** corporation.

For information on translations, please e-mail booktranslations@springernature.com; for reprint, paperback, or audio rights, please e-mail bookpermissions@springernature.com.

Apress titles may be purchased in bulk for academic, corporate, or promotional use. eBook versions and licenses are also available for most titles. For more information, reference our Print and eBook Bulk Sales web page at http://www.apress.com/bulk-sales.

Any source code or other supplementary material referenced by the author in this book is available to readers on GitHub (github.com/apress). For more detailed information, please visit https://www.apress.com/gp/services/source-code.

Paper in this product is recyclable

Table of Contents

About the Author

Dustin K. MacDonald is 10x Salesforce Certified, Nonprofit Cloud Consultant. He holds an Accredited Professional in Einstein Prediction Builder and is currently a Senior Consultant at a midsize Salesforce implementation partner that focuses exclusively on nonprofits and public sector organizations. He is a former Affiliate Professor in Data Science at Eastern University in St. Davids, Pennsylvania, and holds several degrees: Bachelor of Professional Arts in Human Services, Master of Science in Data Science, and Master of Business Administration. Dustin was motivated to write this book because there are no books available on Nonprofit Cloud for nonprofit users who may lack technical knowledge, and the timing is right as Salesforce is increasing its focus on this vertical.

About the Technical Reviewer

Jesse Brown is a self-taught Salesforce architect, evangelist, and fanboy based in Indianapolis, Indiana. As of the publication of this book, Jesse has 16 certifications in the Salesforce platform and is eyeing the Certified Technical Architect examination. Jesse works as the Director of Solutions Architecture at Provisio Partners.

Acknowledgments

I am incredibly grateful to everyone who helped bring this book to fruition: the Apress team including Susan McDermott, Laura Berendson, Gryffin Winkler, Shobana Srinivasan, and others who helped behind the scenes and supported this book throughout its development.

I am also thankful to my colleagues at Provisio Partners and RedTag.pro who inspire me each day, especially my supervisor Hillary Dale, Chief Delivery Officer Kim Collins, CIO Erica Cox, CEO Travis Bloomfield, and some of my amazing coworkers including Frank Nichols, Tom Overland, Sergii Korolivskyi, and Volodymyr Monchak who make magic happen daily.

Thank you to Professor Greg Longo, whose support during my time at Eastern University was invaluable in giving me the confidence and knowledge to pursue this work.

A special thank you to my technical reviewer Jesse Brown, who teaches me something new every day and took time out of his extremely busy schedule to ensure the technical accuracy of this book.

I am grateful to my brother, Jonathan MacDonald, who has always been there to bounce ideas off and who supported this book when it was nothing more than a few bullet points on a notepad.

Finally, the deepest appreciation and thanks go to my wife, Melissa, and my kids, Ray and Rose, who put up with endless late nights and review sessions.

Introduction

If you've picked up this book, it's probably because you find yourself in the role of a nonprofit manager, outcomes and evaluation specialist, consultant, architect, or other professional who is required either to directly perform outcomes measurement and impact evaluation or to set up and supervise systems that do.

Before beginning this learning adventure, it will be helpful to understand how this book came to be. I hold a variety of Salesforce certifications, Accredited Professional badges, a bachelor's degree in human services, and two master's degrees. In all that education, I have never had the opportunity to complete a formal course in outcomes evaluation.

After spending years in all areas of nonprofits and helping them use Salesforce as a consultant, the decision to distill those years of learning in one place about how nonprofits use Salesforce – and there are a lot of them – has led to this book about how you can build a proper impact measurement system.

After completing dozens of implementations across all areas of the nonprofit spectrum including housing, homelessness, economic empowerment, poverty alleviation, intimate partner violence, mental health, crisis intervention, suicide prevention, and more, it's become clear that a well-designed impact and outcomes measurement system quickly pays for itself in your ability to tell a better story to your funders.

During the research process, it has become clear there is a lack of written material for Salesforce. Part of this is a function of the fact that the tech world moves fast, and written material is often out of date by the time it is published. Another reason is that the people busy doing work often don't have the time to sit down and write a book.

There are a few reasons not to be discouraged by this reality as you begin to work through this material.

First, even as specific technical implementation details get out of date, the core functionality remains unchanged. In our case, the principles of outcomes measurement and the process of building a rockstar impact measurement system are the same whether you're using Salesforce, an Access database from 1995, or a completely pen-and-paper system.

In this book, you will learn the skills and how to apply them. Salesforce will help us by making it quicker and more efficient, but rest assured that nothing about the core work of impact measurement and outcome evaluation will be out of date by the time you read this.

Second, although blog posts, website articles, and presentations at Dreamforce (Salesforce's annual conference) are a great way to get information, it is often presented with too little detail to immediately act on it. A book gives you the opportunity to dive deep into both the theory and the practice of the subject at hand so that you have a strong foundation to apply what you learn. That's the purpose of this book and I'm confident you will agree that it is met.

About This Book

Before writing this book, certain assumptions were made about the audience. Making this book useful to the widest group possible without also making it too high level that it would prevent quickly implementing the solutions presented is challenging. Adding the additional hurdle of not making it so technical that a Salesforce end user or even a non-Salesforce nonprofit executive would be locked out trying to read it is a difficult needle to thread, but I think it has been achieved.

Although this book assumes little to no Salesforce knowledge before you begin, many are likely reading because you've been using Salesforce for a while and now want to supercharge your impact measurement. For that reason, the basic Salesforce knowledge needed is presented early, and we dive deeper as the book goes on.

If you are actively using Salesforce and are familiar with Nonprofit Cloud, you can safely skip this first chapter which is an introduction to these topics and walks you through each step from first contacting Salesforce to installing the Nonprofit Cloud tools you will use throughout this process.

At the speed that nonprofits must work, it's rare that you get the opportunity to design a system from the ground up with outcomes in mind. For that reason, all the advice and solutions provided in this book will include options for updating your system to move toward best practices without losing your previous data or work.

The rest of this section will review each of the following chapters. Chapter 2 is a high-level overview of the theory and practice of impact measurement and outcome evaluation. This is a primer for those who may be new to this role or a review for those who may be experienced practitioners that may have been away from the basics for a while.

Chapter 2 also reviews common impact measurement and outcome frameworks to help you decide how to proceed. We review Key Performance Indicators (KPIs) and Objectives and Key Results (OKRs). We also look at a traditional fundraising model of return on investment (ROI), a special method for social value called social return on investment (SROI), and cost-benefit analysis (CBA).

Chapter 3 explores a key aspect to building a new evaluation program. The terms logic model and theory of change are used interchangeably in outcomes measurement, but these are slightly different. They refer to a visual and hypothetical map showing how clients move through one, several, or all your programs or services to achieve the desired outcomes.

Along the way, you will provide inputs such as staff and materials to deliver your programs, and the client will realize outputs which are immediately observable effects from the service(s) you provided. Those outputs translate in the long term to outcomes. We'll spend more time going over outputs and outcomes later in the book.

It might seem that because the logic model comes before other work, it should be placed earlier. This chapter is deliberately placed after the common impact and outcome measurement frameworks chapter because it's helpful if you understand where you need to end up (with a decided-on framework) before you start building your logic model. It's a bit like deciding your driving directions. As the paraphrase from Lewis Carroll indicates, "If you don't know where you're going, any road will take you there."

In Chapter 4, we focus on the elements of a strategic plan and discuss how to identify indicators, collect data, establish baselines and targets, and ensure your data quality and reliability.

In Chapter 5, we take our logic model and outcomes that we decided on earlier and begin deciding how to build them in Salesforce. We won't get too technical in this chapter, but we will talk about some basic Salesforce functionality like objects, fields, and reports. See Figure 1 for a view of the Salesforce Object Manager used for managing objects and fields.

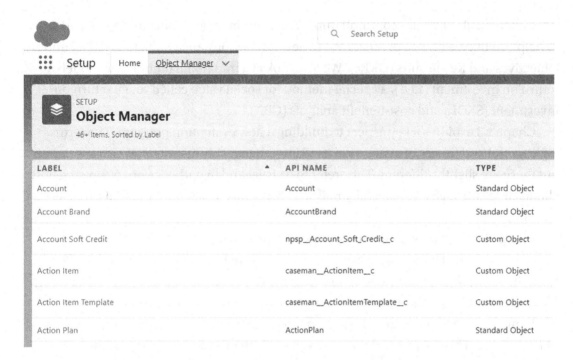

Figure 1. *The Salesforce Object Manager*

Later in the chapter we move from the theoretical to the practical as we look at strategies for collecting data. We'll talk about techniques like paper surveys, Salesforce assessments, Experience Cloud portals, and other methods of getting your output data into Salesforce. We'll also discuss best practices to make sure the data you're collecting is the most robust and reliable.

In Chapter 6, we take the data we've collected and examine how to report out on it. We discuss how to meet the needs of your board, your funders, and the wider community. Integrating your nonprofit impact into your grant proposals is also covered here, as is how to seek out earned media when you have particularly compelling results to share.

In Chapter 7, we focus on the complete change management process, which is used to ensure that individuals are prepared for the changes that your organization implements.

In Chapter 8, we begin wrapping up with three end-to-end case studies to help you understand and apply the concepts throughout the rest of the book. Each case study is based on the outcomes and evaluation work I've done in my career with organizations. The first is a crisis line, the second is a nonprofit Chamber of Commerce, and the third is a homeless shelter and food pantry.

In Chapter 9, we incorporate advanced techniques like Einstein Prediction Builder, Experience Cloud, statistical analysis, and AppExchange solutions to extend the work that you've done by leveraging next-generation technologies.

In Chapter 10, our conclusion, we examine everything you've learned throughout the book and opportunities for you to continue your learning. Good luck and happy learning!

CHAPTER 1

Introduction to Salesforce for Nonprofits

This is a book about conducting impact measurement for nonprofits. If you're reading this book, I assume you work for a nonprofit or an external evaluator or are a consultant like me and are interested in using the power of Salesforce to improve your impact measurement and evaluation. If so, this is the right book for you.

Combine the lack of reading material on subjects related to Salesforce with the lack of resources for nonprofits using Salesforce, and you have a recipe for numerous organizations to not take full advantage of the technology that they've paid very good money for.

This book will help you supercharge your impact measurement and outcome evaluation by developing an understanding of what it means to have an impact and how to measure it. Then we'll learn how to set your Salesforce organization up so that you're automatically collecting the information that you need to be successful. And finally, we'll explore the technologies and techniques you have available to you to best demonstrate the impact you've identified.

By tracing a straight line from your logic model or theory of change, which shows you how the work you do with the people you serve, through to the outputs and outcomes that your clients see, you can tell a more compelling story. And we'll finish by exploring how you can leverage this newfound impact measurement skill to improve fundraising and ensure your organization's long-term success.

We'll close with a set of case studies to demonstrate this process based on several real-life nonprofits I have worked with, including a telephone crisis line, a homeless shelter and associated food pantry, and a Chamber of Commerce.

© Dustin MacDonald 2023
D. MacDonald, *Impact Measurement and Outcomes Evaluation Using Salesforce for Nonprofits*,
https://doi.org/10.1007/978-1-4842-9708-7_1

Salesforce as a platform has been around since 1997. It was created by Marc Benioff with the original slogan – still used today – of "clicks, not code." The Internet was still relatively nascent in the 1990s, and when you wanted most kinds of software, you needed to get them on a CD or, worse, a mainframe. Computer software was big, bulky, hard to use, and often slow to operate. In contrast, Salesforce made the promise of a decentralized workforce something closer to reality by allowing individuals to work from anywhere and allowing sales staff to work at a new office just by visiting a new website.

That original version of Salesforce, called Salesforce Classic, is still available (see Figure 1-1). Eventually, Salesforce transitioned to a new layout and set of code called Lightning. While Salesforce Classic and Lightning work on the same underlying database, Lightning (sometimes also called Lightning Experience or LEX) is a total rewrite of the Salesforce code that takes advantage of modern web standards that, true to its name, often allow you to do things much quicker than you used to.

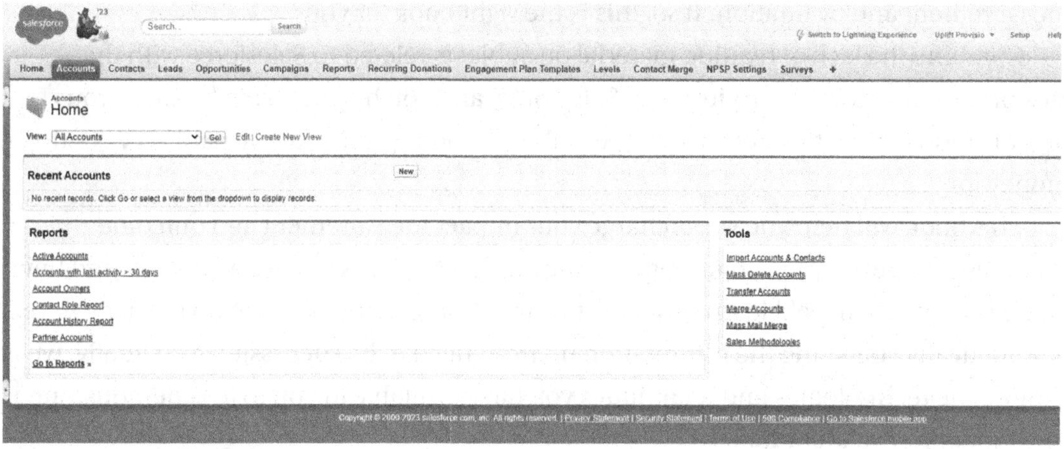

Figure 1-1. *Salesforce Classic*

Salesforce considers themselves a PaaS – a platform as a service. You might hear this referred to sometimes as Software as a Service or SaaS. This refers to an individual software that you can subscribe to, like the Dropbox file storage service.

In contrast, Salesforce provides hundreds of services and technologies inside their platform, like Flows, the Apex programming language, and Experience Cloud Builder, to allow you to create your own extensions to the out-of-the-box functionality.

Each Salesforce product exists as something called a Cloud. When you first subscribe to Salesforce, you will be given access to one of these Clouds. The very first Cloud was called, appropriately, Sales Cloud.

Sales Cloud allows you to do things like add sales leads into the system; record phone calls, emails, and tasks against those leads; convert those leads into Contacts when you've made sales to them; track the Opportunity pipeline from start to end as you make sales; and more. Sales Cloud also includes deal forecasting, which uses the past data you've collected to understand the likelihood of a similar deal closing and allows your sales staff to be as efficient as possible.

Over time, Salesforce added additional Clouds. Some of the most popular include Service Cloud, Health Cloud, Experience Cloud, and Nonprofit Cloud. Service Cloud, one of the earliest Clouds to be launched after Sales Cloud, is designed for service-based organizations or departments. If you are a manufacturer of air conditioners and you use Sales Cloud for your sales staff to work with your suppliers and distributors, your customer service staff can use Service Cloud to help manage customer support.

Service Cloud includes functionality like ticket management via email or through your website, internal and external knowledge bases that can help provide articles and information, and an "OmniChannel" that can allow your support staff to take phone calls, emails, text messages, web-based chats, and more.

Service Console even features AI-powered chatbots using Einstein, which is Salesforce's name for their proprietary artificial intelligence/machine learning technology. These chatbots can reply to common customer issues, and only if it appears the customer's needs lie outside these frequent topics will the chatbot send the chat or text over to a live agent. This all helps to make Salesforce as efficient a tool as possible for support staff.

Health Cloud is another innovative Salesforce Cloud. Developed for the unique needs of healthcare providers like doctor's offices, pharmacies, hospitals, and clinics, Health Cloud allows you to manage the full spectrum of healthcare management including generating 835 and 837P medical billing files, integrating with Electronic Health Record (EHR) systems, and a variety of workflow management tools like Intelligent Form Reader which can read a scanned document and convert it directly to a Salesforce record.

Finally, the Cloud that will be the focus of this book is Salesforce Nonprofit Cloud. You might also hear this product referred to under the umbrella of Salesforce for Nonprofits. This Cloud, like the Clouds mentioned earlier, is made up of a variety of features. Unlike many other Clouds, however, Salesforce for Nonprofits is broken into a few groups of features that Salesforce calls packages. One of those packages is the Nonprofit Success Pack (NPSP). NPSP provides full spectrum donation and grant management to replace or augment donation management software like Raiser's Edge.

Note   We will leverage Nonprofit Cloud for the demonstrations and examples in this book, but you don't need to have Nonprofit Cloud to take advantage of many of the items in this book. The principles and techniques apply equally to all Clouds.

Another package under the Salesforce for Nonprofits umbrella is Nonprofit Cloud Case Management or NCCM. Most of the time when people talk about Salesforce Nonprofit Cloud, this is the big package they are talking about. NCCM provides nonprofits with all the standard case management functionality they need including intakes, checklists, assessments, case plans, and service delivery.

To further add confusion, NCCM is made up of the case management components (sometimes called pure NCCM) and another package called Program Management Module (PMM), as seen in Figure 1-2. PMM is free and provides the ability to add programs and services into Salesforce and track them as you provide support to clients. If you're a small nonprofit, you might use only NPSP and PMM and not need the larger NCCM package.

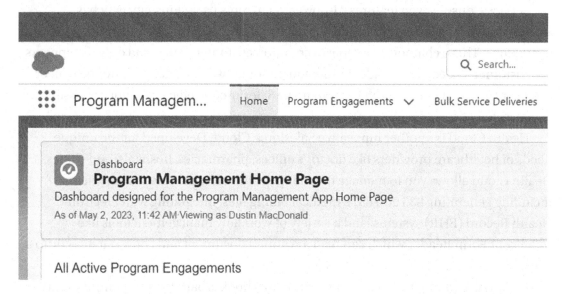

Figure 1-2. *Program Management Module*

The final components of Salesforce for Nonprofits include tools like Outbound Funds, a free add-on used for managing things like administering grants or scholarships on behalf of other people, and Accounting Subledger which is a paid add-on that produces ledger entries for your nonprofit accounting system, shown in Figure 1-3.

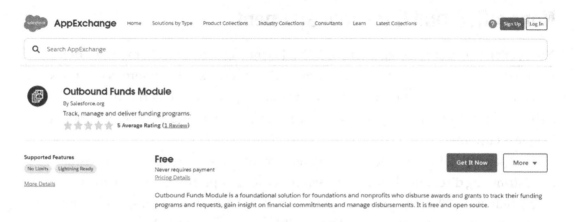

Figure 1-3. *AppExchange listing for the Outbound Funds product*

Throughout this book, we'll look at how you get NCCM/PMM or NPSPS (as your situation dictates) and then how you can leverage these tools for impact measurement. If you happen to use NPSP or another Salesforce Cloud, all is not lost! Most of the things that we discuss are Cloud-agnostic meaning you can learn from them and apply them into your own Salesforce organization.

In addition to these common Clouds, Salesforce has numerous Clouds that go beyond this including things like Auto Cloud for automotive dealerships and GovCloud for federal government customers who have specific compliance requirements. Each Cloud has very specific features. By adding additional Clouds, you can also access new features. For example, Net Zero Cloud includes features and functions that help support organizational efforts to pursue net zero carbon emissions and environmental sustainability.

To choose the right Cloud for you, you'll need to consult your Salesforce Account Executive (AE). Because Salesforce's offerings change all the time, you, and a neighbor who works in Salesforce, even on the same Cloud, may have a different set of services depending on which add-ons you selected.

Introduction to Nonprofit Cloud

This section reviews both Nonprofit Cloud Case Management and the Program Management Module, two major components making up the Nonprofit Cloud in Salesforce.

Nonprofit Cloud Case Management

Nonprofit Cloud Case Management or NCCM is the big behemoth in the Salesforce nonprofit case management world. Before NCCM was released, numerous solutions existed to provide this support. Salesforce was even split into two parts: `https://salesforce.com` was the corporate partner, which licensed the Salesforce platform to business customers.

A separate California Benefit Corporation called Salesforce.org was responsible for distributing discounted licenses to Salesforce for nonprofits and educational organizations. In 2019, the two organizations merged. Salesforce brought the nonprofit components under the aegis of the "mothership" as it's been called.

That same year, Salesforce announced the release of NCCM and Program Management Module (PMM). Until this date, people who wanted to do case management in Salesforce needed to use the Nonprofit Success Pack (NPSP, discussed later) which had no case management functionality and then extend it using a third-party tool from the AppExchange (Salesforce's answer to your phone's app store). Examples of those third-party tools include Birdseye by Provisio Partners and Exponent Case Management by Exponent Partners.

With NCCM and PMM, nonprofits finally had a solution with the weight of Salesforce behind it, and after the merger, nonprofit clients were no longer considered second class citizens. NCCM has continued to evolve, like all Salesforce products in active development, through three-times a year release cycles. These release cycles allow the company to build and trial new features and then release them to all organizations all at once.

In its latest evolution, Salesforce has rolled out a new version called NPC, or Nonprofit Cloud. For more information on NPC, see Chapter 10.

If you've never used NCCM before (or only scratched the surface in your organization), you may be unfamiliar with all the options that it provides.

- **Inbound Referrals**: You can record inbound referrals to understand where clients are coming from and what information you'll need to collect from them before they move to the next stage of working with you.

- **Outbound Referrals**: When you send a client to a community partner, you can track where they went, which program they were referred to, and the person they were referred to. You can also track the status of the referral (was the person able to connect with the agency) and the outcome of the referral (did they get what they needed).

- **Intakes**: Most nonprofits are familiar with the stack of papers that comprise their organization's intakes. An intake is sometimes your first opportunity to collect data from your client and begin understanding their unique needs. In Salesforce, intakes still exist but NCCM Intakes lets you pull data from across your Salesforce system into one page, so you can quickly access it. See Figure 1-4 for an example of an intake.

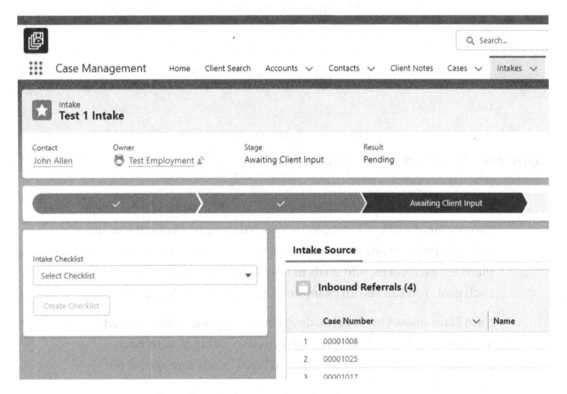

Figure 1-4. *A screenshot showing part of an intake*

- **Intake Checklists**: As part of your intake, you may have a set of digital and paper processes for a client to complete. For example, the client needs to provide you with a paystub or a copy of their ID in addition to filling out some forms. With Intake Checklists, shown in Figure 1-5, you can track these tasks right on the Intake and follow them through to completion.

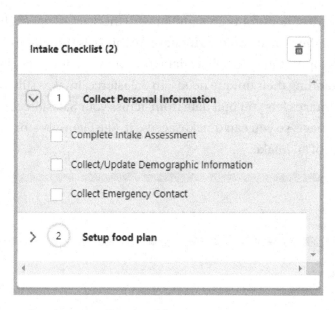

Figure 1-5. *Example of an Intake Checklist*

- **Case Plans, Goals, and Action Items**: Case Plans are a staple of case management work, allowing you to record the goals a client has and their progress toward them. NCCM allows you to create multiple case plans for each client, add goals to them, and then add action items to each goal. You can see an example of a Case Plan in Figure 1-6.

  Case Plans allow you to break down overwhelming goals like "get a driver's license" into achievable steps like "bring in your birth certificate," "read the driver's manual," and "study signage for the written driving test."

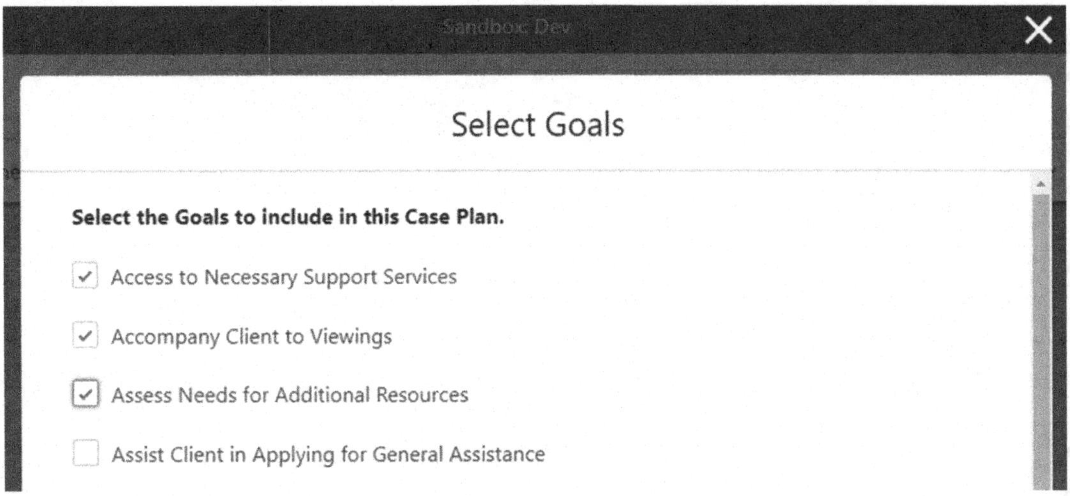

Figure 1-6. *Building a Case Plan for a housing organization*

- **Client Notes**: Client Notes are another common case management requirement. Salesforce supports client notes, which you can save as drafts and submit them later, as well as tagging them so you can quickly find important notes again.

- **Assessments**: Assessments, shown in Figure 1-7, represent a standardized way of collecting information about a client a repeatable basis. Salesforce assessments can be scored, with the results charted over time, compared, and aggregated. We will discuss several examples of assessments later in this book.

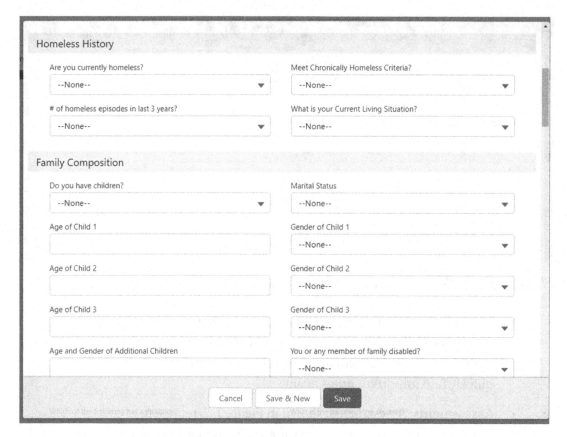

Figure 1-7. *Completing a housing assessment*

- **Reporting and Analytics**: Finally, Salesforce comes with robust
  reporting capabilities. We'll expand on the out-of-the-box reports
  later in this book, but for now, know that Salesforce allows you to
  slice, dice, and report whichever kind of data you need. An example
  of a report is shown in Figure 1-8.

Account Record Type ↑	Account Name ↑	Primary Contact	Total Gifts	Average Gift	Total Gifts Last Year	Billing City	Billing State/Province (text only)
Household Account (23)	Alana Morris Household	Alana Morris	$1,280.00	$160.00	$1,150.00	-	-
	Annie Roberts Household	Annie Roberts	$2,600.00	$650.00	$2,600.00	-	-
	Ann Miller Household	Ann Miller	$25.00	$25.00	$25.00	-	-
	Ben Barnaby Household	Ben Barnaby	$250.00	$50.00	$250.00	Marlboro	California
	Bernie Mac Household	Bernie Mac	$2,000.00	$1,000.00	$2,000.00	-	-

Figure 1-8. *An example report*

You'll notice in that list that there was nothing included about programs or services. This was deliberate, because while NCCM is a paid product, the Program Management Module (PMM) is not. PMM is a free add-on to Salesforce that provides access to Programs and Services functionality and is covered in the next section.

Program Management Module

Program Management Module (PMM) is automatically installed when you install NCCM, if you don't already have it. As a free add-on, however, you can install PMM at any time in any org. PMM allows you to track programs, as the name suggests, and services.

A program represents the service delivery you provide to clients. For example, you might have a counseling program, a food bank program, or a housing program. A service is the kind of support you provide to meet the needs of that program.

Your counseling program might provide mental health counseling or support group sessions as a service. A food bank provides food as a service. And a housing program provides shelter beds. Salesforce lets you set the type and quantity of each service delivery, so you could add one hour of counseling, one group session, or one pound of food to a client's record. By putting clients into program cohorts, you can easily group them, pull them up, email them, and report out on them.

Another major timesaver is a set of features that starts with Service Schedules. A Service Schedule allows you to design a set of recurring service deliveries like a class. You can schedule those and then RSVP people for the individual sessions. Then with a click of a button, you can collect attendance for dozens or even hundreds of people each session. Service Sessions makes managing batch service deliveries a snap.

Nonprofit Success Pack (NPSP)

When people think of Salesforce and nonprofits, especially if they don't work in Salesforce, what often comes to mind is the Nonprofit Success Pack. This is the result of the P10 (Power of Us) program that gives eligible nonprofits ten free licenses to Salesforce with NPSP already installed. This makes it an attractive choice for small or new nonprofits who are dipping their toes into the waters of Salesforce. P10 is discussed later in this chapter.

Although it's free due to the generosity of Salesforce – who hope to make up the revenue as you add additional licensed products and services – NPSP is full-featured and very powerful. It expands and transforms the Opportunity object used for recording information on potential sales so that you can record all kinds of donations including cash, pledges, matching gifts, and in-kind contributions.

Some of the major functionality in NPSP is detailed in the following section.

Soft Credits

By leveraging the power of Soft Credits and Partial Soft Credits, you can give credit where credit is due. If you receive a donation from person A, but it was influenced by person B, you can ensure that person B is counted in their donation totals by using Soft Credits. See a picture of Soft Credits in Figure 1-9.

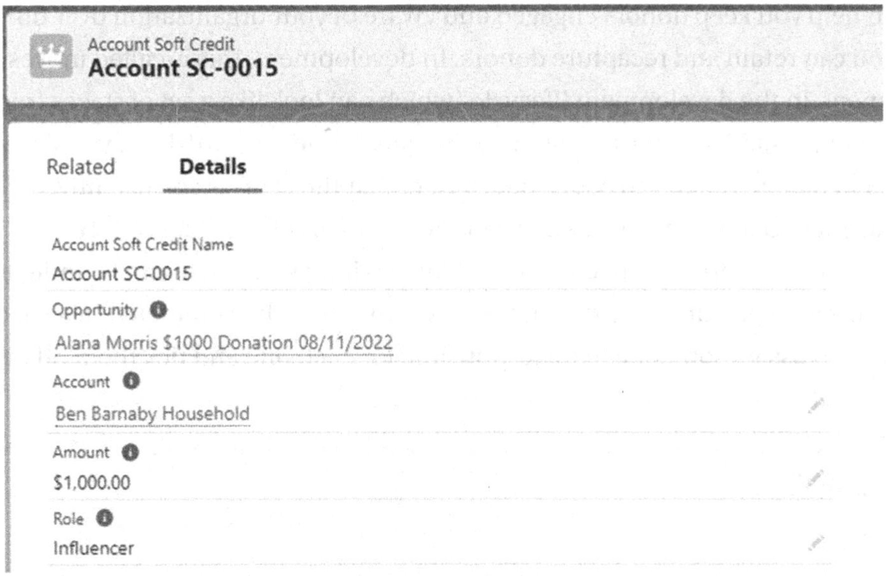

Figure 1-9. *A Soft Credit from an influencer*

Manage Households

The Nonprofit Success Pack allows you to work closely with your donors, who can have situations as complex as the clients that you serve. One of the ways that you can do this is through the Manage Household functionality. If you have two contacts in Salesforce and they move into the same household, you can merge the households together. On the contrary, if a child moves out of their parent's house and is going to be donating or receiving services separately, you can split the new household out from the existing one.

You can also configure settings like the default name of a household, a formal greeting, an informal greeting, and some automation. When you add a new contact into the system, NPSP will create the household using the naming convention you have specified and create a formal greeting with the salutation (e.g., Mr. or Dr.) and full name and an informal greeting using the first name.

Engagement Plans

Like all good fundraising and development staff, you probably have a plan for how to reach out to donors. You'll use this plan to decide when to reach out to new donors, who will reach out to them, and when. For those who have donated in the past, engagement plans can help you keep donors engaged and aware of your organization over time so that you can retain and recapture donors. In development, this is called moves management. In the development lifecycle (which can look like a set of stages from Identification, Qualification, Cultivation, Solicitation, and Stewardship), you'll use engagement plan templates to coordinate and repeat those tasks consistently.

Engagement plans begin life as engagement plan templates (Figure 1-10). Engagement plan templates are created and filled with tasks. Those can be independent tasks that occur at any time and dependent tasks that must be completed in a specific order. You can assign someone to be responsible for each one and tick them off as they are completed.

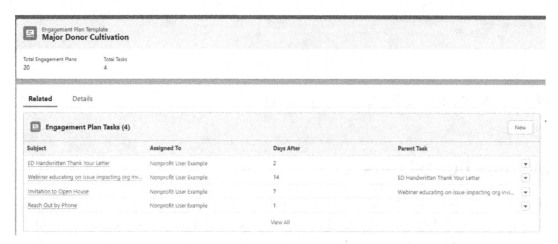

Figure 1-10. *An engagement plan template*

Gift Levels

Gift Levels in Nonprofit Cloud have a few uses. The first is to help you manage your budgeting and your donation activity. For example, if you run a small nonprofit that needs to generate $200,000 a year to operate, you might set up gift levels of

- Gold ($25,000 or more)

- Silver ($10,000 or more)

- Bronze ($5,000)

- Supporter (under $5,000)

If you know that you have two gold level donors, five silver level donors, and ten bronze level donors, you'll know you have brought in $100,000. From your supporters and the wider community, you will need to raise the other $100,000 that your organization needs to operate.

In Nonprofit Success Pack, gift levels will help you track the contribution level of each donor, so you can keep track of their contributions. You can also connect this with automation so that as someone approaches a certain level, such as a Founder's Circle, you proactively reach out to them to encourage them to make that last contribution to push them into the next contribution level and continue to support your organization.

Gift Entry Templates

Nonprofit Success Pack allows you to record all your donations, or gifts as they come in. Because of the unique data that you need to capture for different kinds of donations and different ways of entering those donations, Gift Entry Templates allow you to set up processes that match your preferred workflows.

For example, when adding credit card donations, you might be interested in recording whether those donations are recurring or one-time. If you're adding a batch of donations, you might want a more streamlined data entry process than when you're entering donations once at a time. Gift Entry Templates allow you to handle these different situations to make your donation process the most effective it can be.

Recurring Donations

As a nonprofit, your most loyal supporters are often recurring donors. Whether they give monthly, yearly, or some other frequency, you know when to expect their funds to arrive. This is especially true if they make a pledge and then begin making donations to support the pledge.

Nonprofit Success Pack allows you to handle these recurring donations with ease. You can enter open-ended recurring donations for those donors that have set up a recurring donation schedule or a fixed-length schedule for situations where a person or an organization has committed a specific amount of money that will be disbursed on a regular schedule.

Rollup Summaries

Rollup summaries (often simply called rollups) are one of the most powerful parts of Salesforce. Many users of Salesforce are familiar with rollups from their experience with Master-Detail objects. In a Master-Detail object, one of the objects is the parent and one is the child. By defining a Rollup Summary on the Master object, you can capture the Sum, Count, Minimum, or Maximum of the child records.

For example, if you use Cases to track your inbound and outbound referrals, you might have a Custom Object called Referral Resolution Details that you use for each person who works on that Case to provide information such as the length of time each staff member spends working on the referral by filling out a number field called Duration_of_Work__c with the number of minutes.

If you wanted to know the total number of minutes that all the staff members had spent, you could use a rollup summary to do so. To do this, you would create a field on the parent object, Case, called Total_Minutes_Spent__c, with the field type Rollup Summary and the type set to Sum and the rollup field set to the Duration_of_Work__c field on the Referral Resolution object. Then, for each Case, you would see the sum of the minutes spent from the related Referral Resolution records. Fantastic!

Rollups are great and very powerful. Unfortunately, they have some major limitations. The biggest is that you can only create rollup summary fields on master-detail objects. There is a soft limit of 25 rollup summary fields that can only be raised to a maximum of 40 by Salesforce. While you can have several options for how to summarize (noted earlier), average is not among them.

The Customizable Rollups functionality of Nonprofit Success Pack avoids all these limitations by allowing you to create a variety of rollups including new rollup methods like Average, Distinct (unique values), and Donor Streak which are used to determine the number of years in a row someone has donated.

Reporting and Analytics

Reporting and analytics are some of the most important elements of adopting a Customer Relationship Management (CRM) system like Salesforce. By storing all your data in Salesforce and using it as a single source of truth, you unlock the ability to do advanced reporting to funders, creating and viewing oversight dashboards and more.

Although each component of Salesforce for Nonprofits comes with some pre-created reports and dashboards, learning how to extend this functionality throughout this book will allow you to have confidence that you are doing the right work and demonstrating that to others.

Outbound Funds Module

Outbound Funds Module (OFM) is a newer part of Salesforce for Nonprofits. Started in 2017 and released in 2018 by members of the Salesforce.org community as a free and open source product, it was eventually absorbed by Salesforce in 2020.

OFM remains as a free optional add-on today. It allows you to create funding programs to represent scholarships or other kinds of outbound benefits where funds are being paid directly to constituents. From there, an individual can submit a Funding Request. Finally, you can track requirements such as documents needed, progress reports required, or other steps to manage the funding process.

Finally, the Disbursement object lets you manage the actual payment.

Accounting Subledger

Accounting Subledger allows Salesforce and your accounting system (e.g., Sage or QuickBooks) to talk to each other. When you use Accounting Subledger, the system generates accounting records as standard journal entries. You can use cash or accrual accounting and reconcile accounting periods inside Salesforce in the same way that you do with your accounting system. When you're ready, you can export those ledger entries for import into that external system.

By having matching data in your accounting system and Salesforce, you can take advantage of the power of both systems to be more efficient and have a more unified view of your operations. An example of an Accounting Subledger report is found in Figure 1-11.

Report: Ledger Entries with Opportunity
Sage Intacct Template
Export Ledger Entries to Sage Intacct

Total Records   Total Debit Amount   Total Credit Amount
14              $5,555.00 $5,555.00

	Ledger Entry: Ledger Entry Name ↑	ƒx Journal	Transaction Date	Opportunity: Opportunity Name	GL Code	Debit Amount	Credit Amount
1	LEDG-00000133	GJ	8/11/2022	Alana Morris $1000 Donation 08/11/2022	01-1043-00-00	$50.00	-
2	LEDG-00000134	GJ	8/11/2022	Alana Morris $1000 Donation 08/11/2022	01-1043-00-00	$50.00	-
3	LEDG-00000154	GJ	8/11/2022	Alana Morris $1000 Donation 08/11/2022	Unrestricted	-	$50.00
4	LEDG-00000155	GJ	8/11/2022	Alana Morris $1000 Donation 08/11/2022	Emergency Assistance Fund	-	$50.00
5	LEDG-00000193	GJ	8/11/2022	Katherine Tirabassi $5 Donation 04/04/2023 (8)	01-1043-00-00	$5.00	-
6	LEDG-00000205	GJ	8/12/2022	Louise Overland $100 Donation 04/30/2023 (9 of 10)	01-1043-00-00	$100.00	-
7	LEDG-00000215	GJ	8/11/2022	Katherine Tirabassi $5 Donation 04/04/2023 (8)	Unrestricted	-	$5.00
8	LEDG-00000227	GJ	8/12/2022	Louise Overland $100 Donation 04/30/2023 (9 of 10)	Unrestricted	-	$100.00
9	LEDG-00000238	GJ	8/12/2022	Annie Roberts $1000 Donation 08/12/2022	01-1043-00-00	$100.00	-
10	LEDG-00000248	GJ	8/12/2022	Annie Roberts $1000 Donation 08/12/2022	Unrestricted	-	$100.00
11	LEDG-00000323	GJ	8/28/2022	Sherri Shepherd $250 Donation 04/30/2023 (8)	01-1043-00-00	$250.00	-
12	LEDG-00000335	GJ	8/12/2022	Katherine Tirabassi $5000 Donation 05/01/2023 (9)	01-1043-00-00	$5,000.00	-
13	LEDG-00000350	GJ	8/28/2022	Sherri Shepherd $250 Donation 04/30/2023 (8)	Unrestricted	-	$250.00
14	LEDG-00000362	GJ	8/12/2022	Katherine Tirabassi $5000 Donation 05/01/2023 (9)	Unrestricted	-	$5,000.00
15						$5,555.00	$5,555.00

Figure 1-11. *An Accounting Subledger report*

Other Salesforce Tools

Salesforce includes other packages from Salesforce Labs, which allows Salesforce employees to build and share AppExchange tools with the wider Salesforce community. Examples of apps from Salesforce Labs include Project Management Tool (PMT), which as the name suggests allows you to manage projects, and Salesforce Field Service Starter Kit which extends Salesforce's Field Service product with new Flows and dashboards. Other Salesforce Labs solutions are covered in Chapter 9.

Getting Started with Salesforce

If you've never worked with Salesforce before, this section will help. If you have, you can safely skip this section. If you find yourself interested in adopting Salesforce, the first step is to reach out to Salesforce. You can use the Contact Us page on `https://salesforce.com`, or if you know an existing nonprofit using Salesforce, you can ask for the contact information of their Account Executive or AE.

Either way, once you've established contact with Salesforce, you'll be reached out to by a presales professional who will guide you through the process of signing up for Salesforce. They will create a trial version of Salesforce (also called a trial org) that will be converted to your final version of Salesforce once you finish signing up.

Understanding the Power of Us (P10) Program

For many nonprofits, the Power of Us program, also called P10 for short, is the reason they can afford Salesforce in the first place. This program provides ten free Salesforce licenses to eligible nonprofits. In addition to these free licenses, nonprofits also receive discounts on Salesforce training and events, access to nonprofit user groups to meet like-minded individuals and organizations, and other benefits. The P10 application is shown in Figure 1-12.

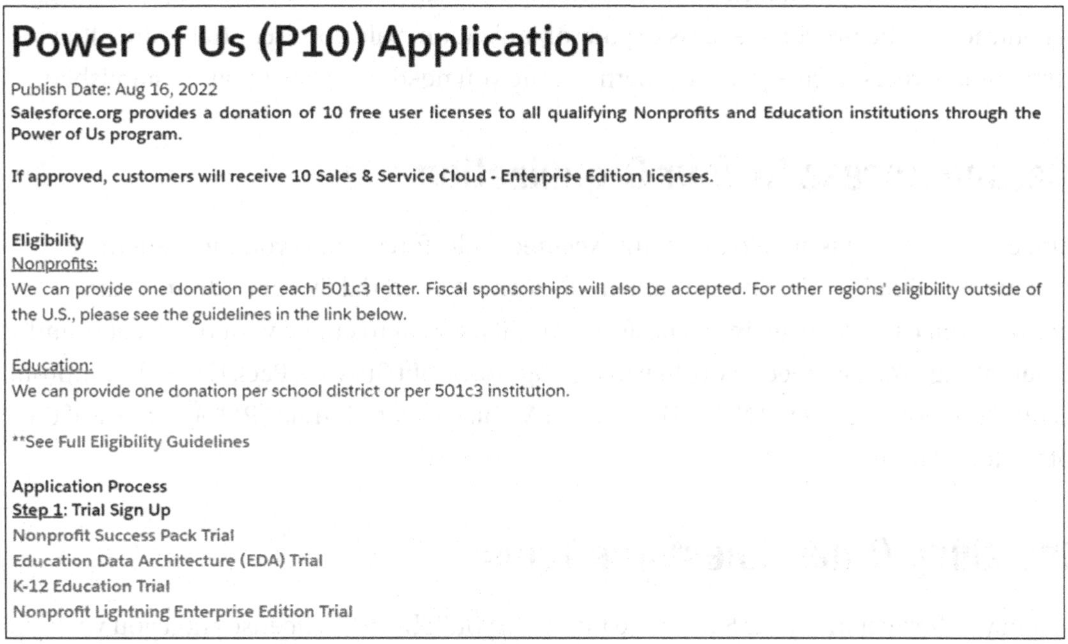

Power of Us (P10) Application

Publish Date: Aug 16, 2022
Salesforce.org provides a donation of 10 free user licenses to all qualifying Nonprofits and Education institutions through the Power of Us program.

If approved, customers will receive 10 Sales & Service Cloud - Enterprise Edition licenses.

Eligibility
Nonprofits:
We can provide one donation per each 501c3 letter. Fiscal sponsorships will also be accepted. For other regions' eligibility outside of the U.S., please see the guidelines in the link below.

Education:
We can provide one donation per school district or per 501c3 institution.

**See Full Eligibility Guidelines

Application Process
Step 1: Trial Sign Up
Nonprofit Success Pack Trial
Education Data Architecture (EDA) Trial
K-12 Education Trial
Nonprofit Lightning Enterprise Edition Trial

Figure 1-12. Salesforce's P10 application page

You'll need to provide some information to Salesforce to support your eligibility. Although the exact eligibility criteria can be adjusted in the future, at the time of printing, the requirements include being an officially recognized "charitable, nonprofit, educational, or social change organization."

You can establish this by pursuing recognition as a tax-exempt organization with 501(c)(3) status as recognized by the Internal Revenue Service (IRS) in the United States or registered charity status with the Canada Revenue Agency (CRA) in Canada.

You can learn more about the Power of Us eligibility requirements at www.salesforce.org/power-of-us/eligibility-guidelines/.

Signing Your Contract

Before you sign your contract, you'll need to meet some specific requirements from Salesforce. These include having an identified System Administrator and authorization from the Executive Director or Board Chair providing approval to sign up for Salesforce. You'll also need to provide proof of your nonprofit status and any other documentation Salesforce needs for your specific situation.

After some back and forth with your salesperson and Account Executive, you'll sign a contract and be provided access to your organization. Salesforce contracts are often for three or five years to give you the length of time you need to get set up and established.

Getting Access to Your Organization

Once your contract is signed and fully executed, Salesforce sends you the credentials to your organization. These will come in the form of an initial System Administrator account you can use to get into Salesforce. You'll use that to create your other users and do anything else you need to do, like installing Nonprofit Success Pack (NPSP), Nonprofit Cloud Case Management (NCCM), Program Management Module (PMM), or any of the other tools you'll use.

Installing Other Salesforce Tools

When you first get into your Salesforce instance, you'll have the licenses that you've purchased or been given in the P10 program. Licenses are only half of the equation. You also need to install the specific apps, features, or functionality that you need.

There are two ways you can do this. The first is using the Salesforce AppExchange. The AppExchange is a marketplace which you can access, even while not logged in to Salesforce, at https://appexchange.salesforce.com/. There, you can search through apps developed by Salesforce and third parties, consultants, and lots of other information.

The other way is to use a special Salesforce tool called MetaDeploy. MetaDeploy is used to install specific collections of code (called packages). Salesforce distributes some packages themselves, and some organizations install code using MetaDeploy.

You can access this using `https://install.salesforce.org/`.

Some of the more than two dozen tools included on MetaDeploy are as follows:

- Nonprofit Success Pack (NPSP)

- Volunteers for Salesforce (V4S)

- Project Management Module (PMM)

- Outbound Funds Module (OFM)

- Nonprofit Cloud Case Management (NCCM)

Conclusion

If you've been following along, you should now have learned a little bit more about Salesforce and the Nonprofit Cloud. If you don't have a Salesforce org yet, you have to sign up for one. Once you've been approved for the P10 program and signed your contract, you've been issued your org with your licenses. Finally, after installing the products you've signed up for, you are ready for the next steps.

In our next chapter, we will review the fundamentals of impact measurement and outcomes evaluation to provide you with the foundation you need to be prepared as you work through the rest of the material.

CHAPTER 2

Introduction to Impact Measurement and Outcome Evaluation

Before we can dive too deep into the practice of impact measurement and outcome evaluation, we need to understand what these things are. We'll start with a review of common definitions, like impact, measurement, outcomes, and evaluation. After that, we'll go into the specifics of each framework that we will be using through the rest of the book with examples. Even if you are someone who has used these frameworks before, it will be valuable to read this chapter, so we have some common definitions to work from as we proceed.

This chapter presents a high-level overview of the theory and practice of impact measurement and outcome evaluation. This is a primer for those who may be new to this role or a review for those who may be experienced practitioners but have been away from the theory.

We will also review common impact measurement and outcome frameworks to help you decide which one makes sense for your specific situation. We review Key Performance Indicators (KPIs) and Objectives and Key Results (OKRs). We also look at a traditional fundraising model of return on investment (ROI) and cost-benefit analysis (CBA).

23

© Dustin MacDonald 2023
D. MacDonald, *Impact Measurement and Outcomes Evaluation Using Salesforce for Nonprofits*,
https://doi.org/10.1007/978-1-4842-9708-7_2

Common Definitions

The first step to overhauling your organization's impact measurement and outcome evaluation is to understand what those things are. **Impact** is the effect that your organization's services or benefits have on the people that you serve. If you are a food pantry, your impact is the food that you provide. If you're a counseling organization, your impact is the counseling sessions that you deliver to community members.

Impact is the first link in a chain that leads to positive social change or difference. If you drop a pebble in the water, that pebble is the impact that you are having on the water.

The next link in this change is the **outputs**. These are the immediate effects that your impact has on the individuals that you serve. In our food pantry example, we provided food to individuals (impact) which caused a reduction in their hunger (output.)

For the counseling agency, the output of their counseling sessions may be a reduced feeling of anxiety or distress or an increased feeling of belonging in the immediate aftermath of the counseling session. Outputs are the first ripples in the water created by the dropped pebble in the water.

Output is often confused with outcome, but these are different, and the distinction is important, especially when we look at frameworks that rely on that difference like social return on investment.

The final link in the chain is **outcomes**. These are the final results or long-term effects of the benefits provided to clients. One way to think about the distinction between outputs and outcomes is to imagine a medical treatment. After surgery, you might be prescribed a painkiller by your doctor. Being prescribed the painkiller is one impact of the physician. Taking the painkiller and having an immediate reduction in your pain is the output.

The reduction in the pain is the part that we can measure and observe: your pain level went from an 8 to a 2. You are feeling much better. The outcome of that pain reduction is that you are now able to participate in activities that you never could before.

Even though participating in those activities is distinct from surgery and painkillers, it is effectively the result of them. This is one of the most important concepts in impact measurement and outcome evaluation. By carefully considering your outputs and how they influence outcomes, you can develop a deeper understanding of your clients and the role your organization plays in their lives. This can help you tell more compelling stories and write better development or fundraising material.

Outcomes represent those ripples very far away; we can't be certain at first glance that they were caused by the pebble we dropped in the water.

It can also help you in your strategic planning because you may choose to focus your organization's activities on services you know are providing the best return on investment or are most in line with the outcomes that you want clients to have, rather than just on those that you are currently funded for, or that people historically with your organization. For more information on strategic planning, see Chapter 4.

The power of having a strong framework and data to back it up is that you can make decisions being confident that you are considering the whole lifecycle – from meeting a potential client through to providing services and finally to them graduating or finishing working with your organization and being better for it.

Other key words in the title of this book include measurement and evaluation.

Measurement is the process of associating numbers to something so that it can be compared. When we count the number of counseling sessions we've provided or the pounds of food distributed, we are measuring those services. We are also measuring things when we ask someone to rate their level of distress, the amount of anxiety, or how long they've been food insecure. Any time we are going from something that is vague or undefined to a more precise quantity, we have measured it. Measurement is therefore a quantitative process.

Evaluation, on the other hand, is more of a qualitative process. When we are evaluating something, we are assessing its quality or importance. When you evaluate your outcomes, you're first determining if they are really the outcomes that trace back to the outputs that you believe they are. A logic model or theory of change, discussed later in this book, can help you determine that.

Second, you are deciding whether those are the right outcomes. Sometimes a nonprofit can achieve outcomes that are good, but not necessarily the ones that they are looking for.

For example, if you are a counseling agency that provides support to people exiting incarceration, you might find that program participants report feeling better positioned for success in their community and not so alone. That's great! However, if the program was funded to ensure people leaving jail or prison have employment and you are not asking them about employment (or worse, you are asking and they are doing no better with employment than people who had not been through the program), then your evaluation has shown that changes need to be made.

Those changes could include seeking out a different funder, reorienting the program around the outcomes that people are experiencing, or changing the nature of the program to better target the desired outcomes. This last change could involve the addition of job coaches, volunteering opportunities, or supported employment that would better prepare those clients for employment.

Now that we have a common language for what we want to achieve and how we want to go about it, we can review the general steps we'll go through to measure our impacts and evaluate our outcomes before we look at the specific frameworks that can be adopted for this.

Impact Measurement

We've talked about impact measurement earlier, which is the idea of associating numbers with a benefit or service. If your nonprofit has been operating for a while, it's likely you have some kind of impact measurement going on, but you may not. The first step is to start counting.

Whatever services you're providing, begin keeping a log or record of them, so you can know how many people you are serving and how many staff are doing this. If you have access to Salesforce, Program Management Module (PMM) can be a great help in this because you can create Programs and map them to Services, as shown in Figure 2-1.

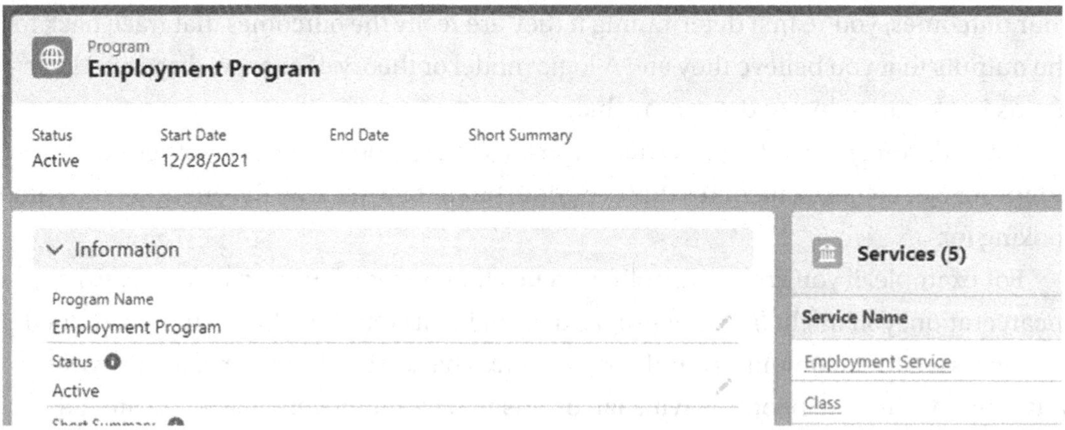

Figure 2-1. *A program record with associated services*

For example, your Counseling program has services called "Counseling Session, Telehealth" and "Counseling Session, In Person." Each time you provide a counseling session, you can record a Service Delivery which includes the details of the counselor, the client, the date and time the service was provided, and other details.

When you are ready to count how many services you have provided, you can use a report like **Service Deliveries by Provider Last Month**, shown in Figure 2-2, to see how many you've provided.

Report: Service Deliveries
Service Deliveries by Provider LastMonth
Which Services did Service Providers spend their time on last month?

Total Records	Total Quantity
3	0.00

Service Provider ↑ ▼	Service ↑ ▼	Service Delivery: Service Delivery Name ▼	Delivery Date ▼	Quantity ▼	Unit of Measurement ▼
- (3)	CSup (3)	Test Test 2023-04-19: CSup	4/19/2023	-	
		Test Test 2023-04-04: CSup	4/4/2023	-	
		Test Test 2023-04-10: CSup	4/10/2023	-	
	Subtotal			0.00	
Subtotal				0.00	
Total (3)				0.00	

Figure 2-2. Sample Salesforce report

Another way to begin measuring your impact is by distributing surveys or assessment tools. We will cover these more in depth later in the chapter. For now, understand that there are numerous validated assessment tools that have been shown to accurately measure different things like anxiety, depression, self-sufficiency, and more.

By integrating these tools into your service provision, you can understand the effect that your services have on a person over time.

Examples of these tools include the following:

- Anxiety: Beck Anxiety Inventory (BAI)

- Depression: Beck Depression Inventory II (BDI-II) or Patient Health Questionnaire-9 (PHQ-9)

- Self Sufficiency: Arizona Self Sufficiency Matrix (ASSM) (see Figure 2-3)

- Most in need of housing: Vulnerability Index - Service Prioritization Decision Assistance Tool (VI-SPDAT)

- Suicide Risk: Ask Suicide-Screening Questions (ASQ)

Domain	1	2	3
Housing	Homeless or threatened with eviction.	In transitional, temporary or substandard housing; and/or current rent/mortgage payment is unaffordable (over 30% of income).	In stable housing that is safe but only marginally adequate.
Employment	No job.	Temporary, part-time or seasonal; inadequate pay, no benefits.	Employed full time; inadequate pay; few or no benefits.
Income	No income.	Inadequate income and/or spontaneous or inappropriate spending.	Can meet basic needs with subsidy; appropriate spending.

Figure 2-3. *The Arizona Self-Sufficiency Matrix*

Some of these tools, like the PHQ-9 or the ASQ, are screening tools that are designed to alert staff of those at higher risk of danger, so they can be provided with more support and deeper assessment. Others like the BDI-II can be administered throughout service provision to understand the improvement in their symptoms over time.

Survey tools are another option. Unlike assessments, these are not necessarily validated tools to collect standardized information on someone's struggles but are instead requests for personal opinions and feelings about the care they've received.

One example that many people have experience with is receiving a customer service survey after they've called a tech support line or reached out for some other kind of assistance. The goal is to collect information about your experience with the specific person or people you worked with and to understand more broadly if there are ways that the experience could be different.

The first written recorded feedback that we know about is from 1750 BCE, when Ea-nasir, a copper merchant, was alleged to have provided substandard product to a customer named Nanni.

The first modern surveys were conducted in the 1830s by the Statistical Society of London to understand the history of strikes, the condition of the poor, and later the state of education. These surveys were done by hand with researchers going door-to-door.

Nowadays, there are numerous survey options including Qualtrics, SurveyMonkey, and even a native Salesforce product called (of course) Salesforce Surveys. With the use of an Experience Cloud, you can also create your own surveys that collect information and put it right into the system. For more information on using Experience Cloud in this way, see Chapter 9.

Outcome Evaluation

Because evaluating outcomes is a qualitative process, it can be more difficult than "simple" impact measurement. Once you've completed the impact measurement process, you'll begin to have some data that you can use to begin your evaluation.

A brief discussion of the logic model or theory of change will be valuable. This concept is covered in depth in Chapter 3. Although they are often used interchangeably (even in this book), there are slight differences between them.

A logic model visually represents your program or service, including the key components, activities, inputs, outputs, and outcomes. It is a linear step-by-step process, which can be used for planning, implementation, and outcome evaluation.

A theory of change goes beyond describing the "what" and instead describes the "why." It traces a line from the inputs to the outcomes and can include multiple logic models or other visualizations to help demonstrate its components. A theory of change can also be used for strategic planning or decision-making about which programs to keep or modify.

Once you have your logic model or theory of change created, you can begin to evaluate the model. Some questions that you may wish to ask yourself include the following:

- Are the final outcomes what your organization wants them to be?

- Do the programs you're offering line up with your agency's mission?

- Do your funders understand and appreciate the outputs and outcomes?

These questions will help you determine if tweaks need to be made to the programs or services to ensure they meet the needs of all stakeholders: staff, clients, funders, and the wider community.

Next, we'll look at some processes that can be used as the overarching frameworks for your outcome evaluation processes. These can help guide your next steps.

Key Performance Indicators (KPIs)

Key Performance Indicators or KPIs are one of the most common ways of measuring success toward a set of goals. Many for-profit organizations use KPIs or OKRs (discussed later) because they are easy to create and understand.

Your organization may already have some KPIs. They are often created as part of a strategic planning or annual review process. These KPIs may be too high level or not relevant to your specific programs, however. If you find yourself without specific KPIs for your program, it is a simple process to come up with them. You can see a KPI dashboard shown in Figure 2-4.

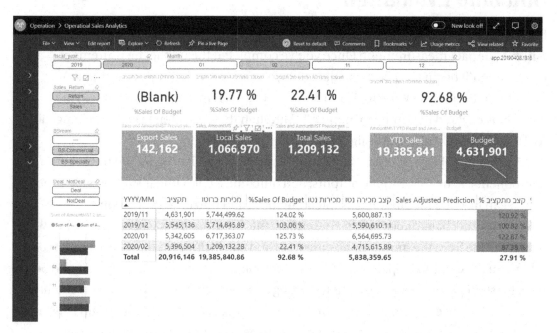

Figure 2-4. *Examples of KPIs from a sales organization, licensed under CC BY-SA 4.0*

SMART Goals

First, understand what is required for something to be a KPI. A common acronym used to describe whether a goal has been written correctly is SMART. This stands for specific, measurable, achievable, relevant, and time-bound.

Specific: For a goal to be specific, it should indicate what the goal is and who should complete it. Rather than saying "handle more crisis calls," you can change that to "send 20% fewer calls to backup services in the next 12 months."

Measurable: A measurable goal is one that has some kind of number attached to it so that you can know whether you have achieved it or not. Looking at the previous example of "handle more crisis calls," how do you define "more"? If you know that you took 10,000 calls last year and you redirected 10% or 1,000 of the calls

Achievable: An achievable goal is one that can be completed. There are a few variations of unachievable goals. One example of an unachievable goal is one that is well-defined, but your organization simply can't reach. Trying to increase your counseling sessions delivered in a year from 500 to 1 million would be too many, too quickly.

The other kind of unachievable goal is one that is too vague to know if you've really achieved it. "Increase the reputation of our program in the community" is a great thought, but it's not something that is easily observable. A more achievable question (that also is more specific and measurable) is "Increase the reputation of our program in the community as reported by the question rating the value of the organization from 1 to 10 in the yearly survey."

Relevant: A relevant goal is one that is related to your program. If you run a counseling program, making your KPIs based on the number of counseling sessions you deliver is great. Making KPIs based around the number of people who visit the website is not as great because it does not help you know if you are meeting your actual goals.

By having relevant goals, you ensure that you continue to track progress toward things that are meaningful for the organization.

Time-bound: A time-bound goal is one that has a time attached to it. If you don't put a timeline on something, you'll have less pressure to achieve it and be unable to know if you ever did. By adding a time-bound to your goal, you can definitively say whether that goal was achieved or not. A common time period used is a year, or the length of your strategic plan which may be one to three years, whichever comes first.

Steps to KPI Process

There are several suggested steps for creating KPIs. The set of steps that I like is as follows:

1. Identify outcomes.

2. Define success.

3. Select a measure for each element of success.

4. Set a target.

5. Begin measuring.

6. Assess results.

We'll look at each of these in depth.

Identify Outcomes

The first step to creating KPIs is, paradoxically, to understand the final result. If you don't know where you are going to end up, you will have trouble choosing the right one. The goals you came up with in the previous step can be helpful for this, as can looking at your organization's mission and vision.

These outcomes can include things like the following:

- Reduce food insecurity in our community.

- Decrease the suicide rate among teenagers.

- Improve the economic situation in the county.

You'll note that these are not SMART goals. And that's okay, because in the process of creating KPIs, we go from this ill-defined endpoint and work our way back.

Define Success

The second step is to understand exactly what numbers are required to achieve the outcomes you determined in the previous step. This is where you put the numerical elements to the outcomes. For the goal of reducing food insecurity in a town, you need to understand what the current rate of food insecurity is. For that, you could consult the Household Food Security in the US survey administered by the US Department of Agriculture (USDA)'s Economic Research Service (ERS).

For the suicide rate, you could look to the CDC's National Vital Statistics System (NVSS) which tracks mortality among different causes, age ranges, genders, and other populations.

To understand the economic situation in the county, you could examine the employment rate as collected by the Department of Labor or data on the number of businesses from the Secretary of State.

The running theme here is that there is a source of data out there that will allow you to understand if the thing you want to achieve is changing. Once you've determined that, you can begin to create measures.

Select Measures for Each Element of Success

Now that you understand the final outcomes, you can begin selecting measures that will help you get there. These measures can be the SMART goals that you created earlier. Returning to our three example outcomes earlier, here are some example measures that could be part of KPIs:

Reduce food insecurity in our community.

- Number of pounds of food distributed
- Rate of food insecurity as measured by the USDA ERS
- Number of clients served by the food pantry

Decrease the suicide rate among teenagers.

- Number of suicide attempts or suicide deaths
- Calls to the teen crisis line
- Hours of counseling provided

Improve the economic situation in the county.

- Unemployment rate as measured by the Department of Labor
- Clients assisted with resume writing or career skills
- Number of businesses in the county

You'll note that these are not always directly related to the program at hand. For example, calls to a crisis line are not directly related to the suicide rate. At the same time, the number of calls provides the opportunity for active rescue of suicidal individuals which can reduce the teen suicide rate.

In this way, a variety of interrelated measures can help you reach the ultimate outcome that you are trying to impact.

Set a Target

Once you've decided on the measures that are important to achieve the outcomes that you are interested in, you can also collect the data on the baseline rate for those items that are measured by outside parties.

The U6 unemployment rate as reported by the Department of Labor includes individuals who are unemployed but also those who are discouraged (unemployed and not looking because they believe there are no jobs to find) and underemployed (those not working enough hours.)

The U6 unemployment rate across the country in February 2023 was 6.8%. You may say that you want your community's unemployment rate to be reduced by 10% in the next year. This would put the rate at 6.12%.

If you had provided 400 hours of counseling last year, you might say that you want to provide 500 hours this year, or a 20% increase.

Begin Measuring

After you've identified a goal and a target, you can begin capturing the data to track your progress. As discussed previously, Salesforce's PMM makes this easy using Service Delivery records.

If you use Salesforce to take phone calls, you'll also have Task or Voice Call records for each call that you can use to collect this data. Other objects like Case, Program Engagement (from PMM) or Intake (from NCCM) can be used to store the data that you will use to measure data.

Salesforce provides several ways to ensure that your data is robust. By making fields required, they must be completed when that record is created.

Validation rules in Salesforce use formulas or expressions to evaluate a piece of data and prevent you from including invalid or false data.

For example, if you have a date field called Date Consent Form Signed (Date_Consent_Signed__c), you may want to make sure that the consent form is not listed as being signed earlier than the date the Contact record was created - because you don't create the Contact record before you have had contact with the client. If this data is entered this way, it must have been an error or a typo.

This validation rule, created on the Contact object, might look like the following:

```
Date_Consent_Signed__c < Contact.CreatedDate
```

In this case, if the date the consent form was signed is earlier than the date the contact is created, an error will be thrown. For more information on validation rules, see Chapter 5.

Assess Results

Once you've captured your data, you can begin assessing the results. Salesforce reports and dashboards are a great way to begin assessing your performance toward the goals that you've set.

With dashboards, you can include a variety of charts including line charts, bar charts, scatterplots, and gauges and KPIs which report single numbers. By configuring the ranges, you can quickly see whether the results are approaching or achieving the results that you want or falling short.

Objectives and Key Results (OKRs)

Objectives and Key Results (OKRs) are like KPIs but not identical. OKRs set up the objectives or the outcomes that you want your organization or program to achieve. In this way, they are like the first step of the KPI process, rather than the final result.

After identifying the objectives that you want to achieve, you then move on to identifying key results. These are the things that you will achieve. For example, if the objective is to increase the number of counseling sessions you deliver, key results might include the following:

- Take out four advertisements in the newspaper and seek out two earned media appearances.

- Hire two additional counselors.

- Adopt a scheduling tool by Q2 to ensure clients are notified about their appointments.

These key results have similar elements of SMART goals, but they are specific achievable activities that the organization or program will embark on, rather than describing the end goal.

One way that Salesforce can help you track the progress toward these key results is using task records which can be assigned to users, associated with other records in

Salesforce (like Notes, Service Deliveries, or even custom objects like a Media Outreach object used to track approaches to journalists.) You can see a task record in progress in Figure 2-5.

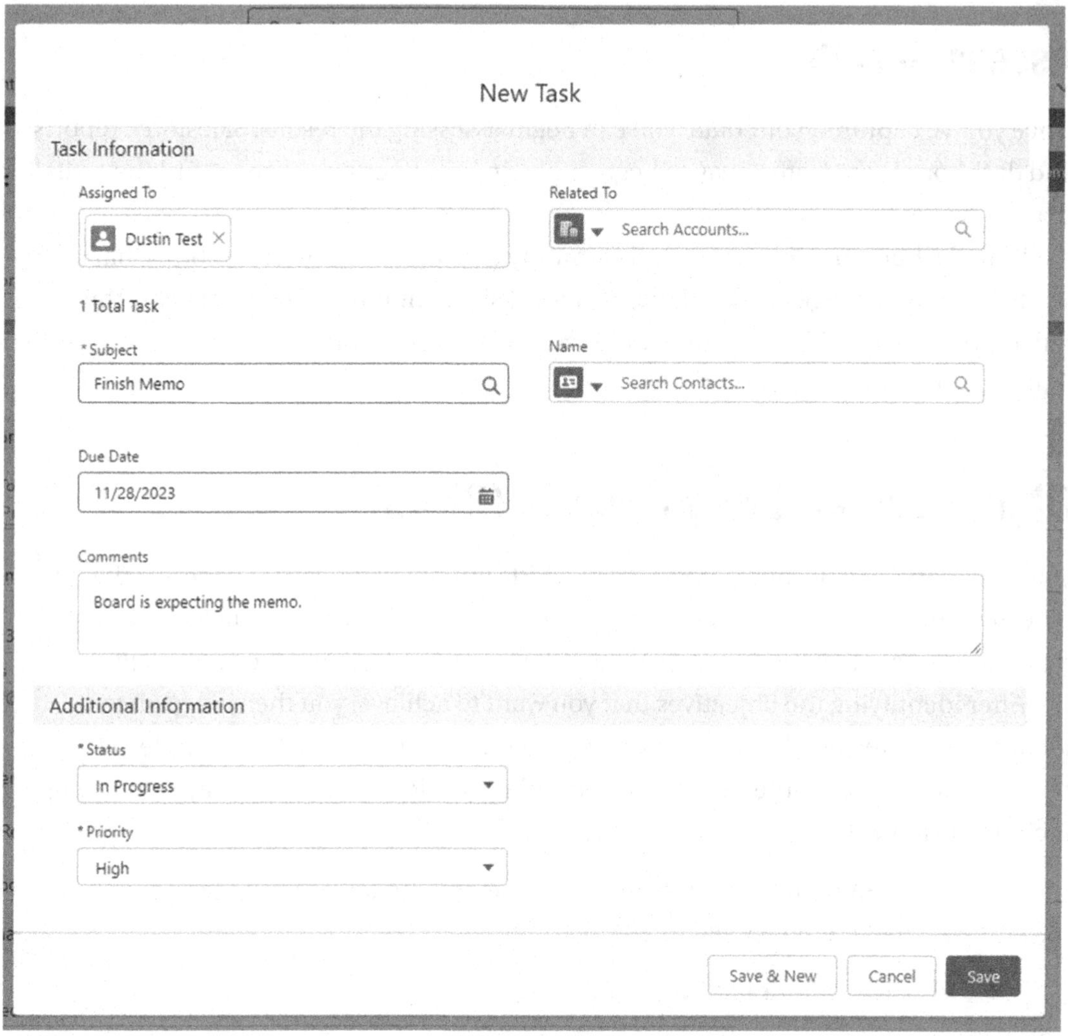

Figure 2-5. *A task record being created*

You might wonder whether to choose KPIs or OKRs. The answer is simple: whichever one seems to be a better fit for your processes. If you prefer to focus on the end result and work backward, KPIs are probably the better option.

If you would prefer to know what tasks you need to complete, more like a checklist, then OKRs may be the better option.

Return on Investment

In contrast to KPIs and OKRs, the next frameworks we will look at are more quantitative than qualitative. The first of these quantitative chapters is return on investment or ROI. This term is thrown around a lot when people talk about the benefits that result from any amount of money spent, but the technical sense has a slightly different definition.

In the first definition, the ROI is calculated as the amount of benefits or services that are created or delivered, divided by the money that is used to create those benefits or deliver those services.

If you have a nonprofit that has a budget of $250,000 and provides 118,000 pounds of food at a food pantry, then the cost per pound is about $2.12. This is dividing the $250,000 by the 118,000 pounds of food. Similarly, 118,000 divided by $250,000 is 0.472 pounds of food for each dollar that is invested.

These 118,000 pounds are the return on investment from the money that was raised.

The second definition is purely financial. Based on the fundraising expenses the organization has, how much money did they bring in? This is the accounting definition of return on investment. If the organization mentioned earlier has $250,000 in revenue but they paid a development director $50,000 a year to raise that $250,000, then the ROI is $250,000 / $50,000 or 1:5. For each dollar invested in fundraising, there is $5 brought into the organization.

Neither method of ROI may capture all the things that the organization does. For example, they may have provided 5000 referrals. These referrals are more intangible, however, and are better measured with social return on investment, covered next.

Social Return on Investment

Social return on investment (SROI) is a useful and innovative tool for nonprofits that goes beyond the usual financial return on investment to capture the value of the intangibles that an organization brings. By adding the amount of intangible social value created and dividing it by the cost of delivering those services, you get a much more complete picture of the real value your organization delivers.

An SROI ratio from a report I wrote is shown in Figure 2-6.

Figure 2-6. *An SROI ratio from a report*

SROI has six major steps:

1. Establishing the scope and identifying stakeholders

2. Mapping outputs

3. Demonstrating outcomes and giving them a value

4. Establishing impact

5. Calculating the SROI ratio

6. Reporting, using, and embedding the SROI

Establishing the Scope and Identifying Stakeholders

In the first step, you decide what program or programs the SROI analysis should cover and identify who can provide the information needed for the later steps. Stakeholders represent the people who are affected by the benefit or service such as the clients, the service providers, and others at the agency - but also the wider community.

You may not be aware of all the stakeholders up front, so a "snowball" may be helpful where you identify each of the stakeholders that you can think of and then go to those stakeholders and ask them who they think are the stakeholders.

After talking to enough people, you'll find that you're getting the same answers and you can then start to narrow the list to the stakeholders that are most impactful in your analysis. For example, although the families of your clients are stakeholders, the benefits they receive may not be distinct enough to include.

The other thing to understand is that when you go to build a logic model, you will want to consult your stakeholders wherever possible, because they are often the ones who have direct knowledge of how they benefited from your services. This is especially important for organizations which serve marginalized populations like food banks, crisis lines, and counseling organizations because their lived experience is going to be incredibly important in ensuring that you have the right approach.

Once you have your stakeholders and the explanations from them about how the program or service helped them in the short term (outputs) and long term (outcomes), it's time to map those outputs and outcomes together, so you can understand which short-term outputs feed into the long-term outcomes.

Mapping Outputs

By mapping outcomes, you take each of the benefits identified by the stakeholders and map them to the outputs that you provide.

For example, a crisis line provides crisis support. During these crisis phone calls, the immediate outputs are that the caller's distress level goes down. They feel more connected to other people. You may even de-escalate a suicidal crisis and prevent them from attempting suicide.

These immediate outputs are what you know you have delivered. The food bank's immediate outputs are the food they give to people and the reduction in their hunger for that day, week, or month.

These outputs are the base value, or the tangible value that you can measure. In an ROI situation like looked at earlier, this is all that you would be able to track. However, there is an intangible social value that is created. This is most easy to understand when we look at the diversion from other services that is caused by your organization.

Returning to our crisis line example, there are two possible scenarios for someone in a suicidal crisis. In the first, the crisis line doesn't exist, or they otherwise can't access it.

They attempt suicide. They call 911, and two paramedics respond in one ambulance to take them to the hospital, which costs $600. They spend an average of 7.74 days there at a cost of $998 a day, plus the $249.36 that the paramedics cost.

Without even getting into the person's lost wages and other possible losses, the cost to respond to a suicide attempt is at least $8000. (Some of the math has been simplified, and these are Canadian dollar figures, but the concept is the same.)

The other scenario is that the crisis line does exist, and the caller is able to get the support that they need. The crisis line worker provides immediate support and de-escalation. The caller still goes to the hospital via ambulance, so the health system incurs the $849.36 cost for the ambulance and paramedics, but they only stay one night. The total cost to respond to this suicidal crisis is $1,847.36.

The difference between the $8000 that the suicide attempt could have cost the system and the $1,847.36 (which is $6,152.64) that it did cost is the social value. It's not visible in the figures that either the crisis line or the hospital incurred but rather is visible in what they *didn't* spend.

This is the beauty of SROI. Every counseling appointment that is avoided, every police or ambulance call that is prevented, or every incarceration that is diverted is social value – as is the value of providing someone with a better quality of life, reducing their illnesses, extending their lifespan, and a myriad of other benefits that are intangible but valuable.

Demonstrating Outcomes and Giving Them a Value

At this fictional crisis line based on one that I have been involved in, Salesforce's Service Cloud Voice is integrated with Amazon Connect.

When individuals in distress call in, they are instantly connected to an available responder. A Voice Call record opens immediately that shows their call history if they have called in before, and the crisis worker opens a Case record to record narrative details of the situation and select their interventions (responses) and the result or disposition of the call.

Some of the results or dispositions that the crisis worker can select include the following:

1. Decreased harmful intentions

2. Immediate crisis diffused

3. Decreased suicidal intent

4. Improved self-esteem, self-control, or confidence

5. Less distressed or anxious

6. Options explored

7. Action plan explored

8. Active Rescue provided (suicide attempt in progress stopped)

These are the outputs because they are directly measurable or attributable to the work the crisis worker did on the phone. The long-term outcomes are a little different.

For the first three

- Decreased harmful intentions

- Immediate crisis diffused

- Decreased suicidal intent

The final outcome is reduced use of 911. In this situation, the crisis was defused, and the individual did not need to go to the hospital.

For the next four

- Improved self-esteem, self-control, or confidence

- Less distressed or anxious

- Options explored

- Action plan explored

The final outcome is improved caller coping skills. The individual feels more able to cope with their day-to-day life and experiences a decrease in their level of distress or anxiety. This is a supportive benefit of many crisis lines.

For the final output in this example

- Active Rescue provided (suicide attempt in progress stopped before action taken)

The final outcome here is reduced use of the healthcare system. This is the outcome that matches the example we discussed earlier, where the individual goes to hospital but without having taken action to end their life yet.

The next step after mapping out the outputs and outcomes is to give them a value. This involves associating a financial proxy with each of the outcomes. Remember the stakeholders you identified in the first step? Here is where they become extremely valuable.

For some outcomes, you can clearly calculate them, like the ambulance example we discussed earlier. For others, like "improved caller coping skills," you may need to talk to your stakeholders about what they would do if they didn't have the crisis line to talk to. They might consider an hour of talking to a crisis line equivalent to an hour of talking to a counselor, going to some kind of leisure activity like a movie (which many people find reduces their anxiety), or some other action that you can put a dollar value on.

There are numerous sources of financial proxies out there. Some include databases maintained by Social Value UK, research articles, and other SROI analyses that have been conducted.

Establishing Impact

For the three outcomes we identified earlier, let's look at some potential proxies. For the first one, reduced use of 911, a proxy can be the cost of an ambulance ride to the hospital and a 3-hour hospital stay to receive crisis de-escalation.

The ambulance and workers cost $849.36 (see previous for the math on that one.) The $998 per hospital stay per day, prorated to three hours, is ($998 / 24 hours) x 3 hours = $124.75.

The final avoided cost is $849.36 + $124.75 = $974.11. For each situation where a high-risk caller is de-escalated over the phone and does not need to go to the hospital, there is a social value created of $974.11.

For the second outcome, improved caller coping skills, through a discussion with stakeholders, they explain that a call to the crisis line helps them feel better for at least a day. Since the median amount spent on leisure per year is $3922 and we prorate that to one day, we have $3922 / 365 = $10.75. For each caller who experiences increased coping skills, we have generated $10.75 in social value.

Finally, for the third outcome, reduced use of the healthcare system, we have the $6,152.64 that we calculated in the previous section in this outcome. Now each of our outcomes has a value.

If we assume that we had 50 calls where we reduced use of 911, 12 active rescues where we reduced use of the healthcare system, and 500 calls where we increased coping skills, the amount of social value we generated is as follows:

- 250 x $124.75 = $31,187.50

- 50 x $974.11 = $48,705.50

- 9700 x $10.75 = $104,275.00

The total of these three is $184,168 in social value. Next, we'll look at how to calculate and use the SROI ratio.

Calculating the SROI

The SROI value is usually expressed as a ratio. You take all the inputs, or the resources that it takes to deliver the program, and you divide them by the social value that is generated.

In this fictional crisis line example, we take about 10,000 calls a year and we generate $184,168 in social value.

Assuming we have two staff, an executive director who makes $40,000 a year and a program director who makes $30,000 a year, plus rent, utilities, and fundraising of $10,000 a year, our inputs are $80,000. In this example, the actual direct support is provided by a team of volunteers, so the input costs are minimal.

In fact, volunteers are social value generators themselves. A trained social services volunteer can often replace a skilled staff person who makes $24 an hour or more and therefore improve your SROI ratio significantly. In this case, though, we'll stick with the value produced only by this subset of calls.

By dividing our social value of $184,168 by the inputs of $80,000, we arrive at the number $2.30. This means that for each dollar invested in the program, we generate $2.30 of social value.

There are other ways you can adjust your SROI value as well. These are known as attribution, deadweight, and sensitivity analysis.

Attribution involves reducing the value of the social value by removing what portion depended on others. For example, if you receive referrals from another organization, you may want to reduce your social value around connection because some of that feeling of connection was provided by the first organization.

Deadweight involves reducing the value of the social value by the percentage that would have happened anyway. Your stakeholders can explain how they would have coped without the benefit to see if there is a need to estimate deadweight.

Finally, a sensitivity analysis involves taking a higher and lower estimate of the final value to have a more tempered estimate to rely on, rather than assuming that the value you calculated is the absolute.

There are other concepts like drop-off (the reduced effect of the intervention over time) and displacement (how providing social value in one area causes an increase in issues in other areas) that are outside of the scope of this book.

Reporting, Using, and Embedding the SROI

The final step is to report and use your SROI value. It can be incorporated into your marketing and fundraising materials, in grant applications, and when seeking other sources of funding.

One way to take advantage of an SROI calculation is to send a press release to the local paper. You can also distribute these materials on your website or other printed materials.

As you begin to build your own database of financial proxies in your area of expertise, you may also wish to distribute these to other nonprofits that are doing similar work. This can help build your organization's thought leadership and help improve the quality of these proxies as you work with collaborators to ensure the values are the most effective they can be.

Cost-Benefit Analysis (CBA)

Cost-benefit analysis is another quantitative form of program evaluation. In this case though, it is a combination of the ROI and SROI methods that were discussed previously.

CBA attempts to consider both the quantitative and qualitative elements. Or put differently, it tries to capture all the benefits – both financial and social – against all the costs.

Adapting our previous examples slightly, we have a small crisis line that has inputs of $80,000 and social value of $184,168. At the same time, the fundraising expenses for this organization are $5,000.

- $80,000 / $5,000 = 1:16 ratio, or a very strong return on investment

- $184,168 / $80,000 = $2.30, or a reasonable social return on investment

Generally, you should use the metric that makes sense for your specific situation or that your funder asks you to use.

Pre-Post Comparison

Pre- and post comparison is a method of evaluating a program by looking at the results on a survey or assessment tool before an individual has gone through the intervention (in this case, the program or service) and after to see the change.

One way this can be achieved is by completing an assessment like the Beck Depression Inventory before and after the service delivery to see if the individual's depression has changed.

Another option is to ask callers to a crisis line or other service what their level of distress is at the beginning of the conversation and then to ask again after they've spoken to the crisis worker. For web chats, this can be automated using a tool like Service Cloud's pre-chat and post-chat pages.

Conclusion

In this chapter, we have looked at several methods of impact measurement and outcome evaluation, including qualitative methods like KPIs and OKRs and more quantitative methods like ROI, SROI, CBA, and pre- and post-measurement.

In the next chapter, we will explore the process of building a logic model and theory of change so that we can understand the ways in which our programs are affected before we begin building our data model inside Salesforce.

CHAPTER 3

Creating Logic Models and Theories of Change

In the previous chapters, you received a thorough overview of the functionality key to both basic Salesforce and the Nonprofit Cloud and a necessary grounding in impact measurement and outcome evaluation that will be necessary for the remainder of your reading.

Now it is time to walk through the process to craft a logic model or theory of change. Because a theory of change is more comprehensive than a logic model and may contain multiple logic models, we will use this as the structure for our work together.

An example of a logic model created by Wikimedia is shown in Figure 3-1.

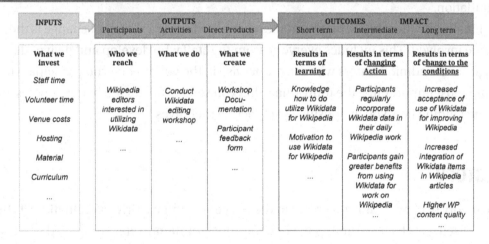

Figure 3-1. *A logic model created by Wikimedia, used under the Creative Commons Attribution-ShareAlike 4.0 license*

© Dustin MacDonald 2023
D. MacDonald, *Impact Measurement and Outcomes Evaluation Using Salesforce for Nonprofits*,
https://doi.org/10.1007/978-1-4842-9708-7_3

As a reminder, a theory of change is a complete review of the assumptions, beliefs, and causal links that allow your program to achieve the desired outcomes. By combining the theory of change with a logic model, you have a self-contained tool that can be used to ensure that the effects that you desire to happen from your program, service, or intervention do.

To ensure that your theory of change is valid, you will need to consult a wide range of stakeholders and other resources. These can include scientific literature, gray literature, and individuals.

Scientific literature includes studies published in peer-reviewed journals that have empirically evaluated inputs and outputs but also conference proceedings and papers and books published by academic presses. These can be good references for well-established programs or techniques that have existed long enough to be deeply researched.

Gray literature contains a variety of formally published material that happens to be outside of commercially published work for profit (which is called white literature) and scientific literature that is peer reviewed. Gray literature includes research reports, other program evaluations, white papers that discuss programs like yours, and material published by government organizations like the Substance Abuse and Mental Health Services Administration (SAMHSA) and the National Institutes of Health (NIH) and think tanks like the Brookings Institution, Rand Corporation, and the Heritage Foundation.

Finally, the most important resource when developing a theory of change is the people involved. This includes everyone from the staff who develop and deliver the program, the administrators who may supervise it, the volunteers who participate in it, and most importantly, the individuals that you serve who are the best resources for understanding how you are positively impacting their lives.

History

The theory of change draws its roots to the concept of theory-driven evaluation (TDE) which itself goes back to the 1930s when the educator Ralph Tyler completed what is now called the Eight Year Study (1933–1941) to examine the link between high school curriculums and outcomes.

This approach solidified some basic concepts that are still used in program evaluation today: the importance of having a theory to base your experiment or evaluation on so that you understand what should happen, the importance of testing the same population over time, and the value of incorporating changes learned as a result of what was learned.

Although Tyler represented the genesis of evaluation, the term theory-driven evaluation (TDE) was coined in Huey-tsyh Chen's 1990 book *Theory-driven Evaluation*. Expanding on material from a 1989 article in the journal *Evaluation and Program Planning*, Chen set out to demonstrate that by building a framework to understand how a program should work in theory, you can ensure that your program actually does what you expect it to and, if it does not, to understand what scientifically validated changes are necessary to ensure it will.

Before TDE, programs were developed based on gut feelings or a primitive understanding based on observing other programs but without a deep understanding of how they worked. When it came time to evaluate a program, before-and-after or input-output program designs could be used that would show the program made a difference, but without demonstrating conclusively why the change occurred.

The result was programs that worked in some geographies, populations, or time periods were duplicated in others and less effective. This leads to a waste of funder dollars and a hit to the confidence of motivated program staff and administrators.

The 1995 book *New Approaches to Evaluating Community Initiatives: Concepts, Methods, and Contexts* (shown in Figure 3-2) was published by the Aspen Institute, a think tank whose Roundtable on Community Change featured the work of Carol Weiss. In the book, Weiss explained how program evaluation is difficult or impossible to accomplish when the assumptions underlying the changes are unknown, unstated, or poorly supported. It was Weiss who named this process the theory of change.

Figure 3-2. *A seminal book in program evaluation*

By clearly laying out all of the assumptions, beliefs, and steps that an individual or group will proceed through when receiving some kind of benefit or service, you can ensure that those benefits are actually realized and intervene to keep individuals on track as they move from the smaller goals to the big ones that are the ultimate reason for the program to exist.

A theory of change is a necessary component for some of the frameworks we have discussed. For example, if you are completing a social return on investment (SROI) evaluation, you must have a theory of change to understand the outputs that lead to the desired outcomes.

For many other program evaluation methods, a theory of change is not required but it is extremely beneficial. For program staff who deliver or supervise a program, building a theory of change will help them better understand the meaningfulness of the work that you do and more expertly target your interventions to ensure the maximum success for your clients.

For administrators, executives, and development staff, having a theory of change will help them better talk about your mission, craft more compelling fundraising messages, and recruit staff who truly believe in what your organization does because you can demonstrate it empirically.

Finally, for Salesforce consultants, IT staff, business analysts, and architects, a theory of change will help ensure that you are discovering, designing, architecting, and building a system that allows end users to collect the information they need.

Although you may not necessarily be the person who is building the theory of change, by understanding how one is built and what each component is used for, you will be better prepared for whichever role you will play in the impact measurement and outcome evaluation process.

Steps to Creating a Theory of Change

There are several models or frameworks for creating a theory of change. Each one breaks the process down into a series of manageable steps that can be accomplished to go from a disparate set of information to a completed, grounded, effective theory of change. These range from 4 to as many as 20 steps.

The ten steps outlined here are based on the model developed by New Philanthropy Capital, a British thank tank and consultancy. A brief review of these ten steps is as follows, and working through them in-depth will form the rest of the chapter.

Issue Analysis

In issue analysis, the goal is to develop a comprehensive understanding of the issue that you are setting out to solve. For a food bank, this would involve developing an understanding of food insecurity. For a crisis line, understanding what factors underpin suicidality or poor mental health. For an environmental advocacy organization, what causes someone to participate or not participate in activities that help climate change?

If this is an issue that your organization has dealt with for a while, this shouldn't be too challenging. If this is a new area for you though, it may take you some time to get a strong understanding of the issue at hand.

One of the most important elements from a program evaluation perspective is to ensure that you are not "boiling the ocean." This means that you shouldn't try to solve every facet of an issue. A lack of specificity and focus will dilute your efforts. By focusing your program, and more importantly your evaluation, on a single area, you will have a stronger evaluation.

Sources for your issue analysis can include many of the resources discussed previously: government agencies, think tanks, scientific journal articles, and other nonprofits working in the same issue area.

At the same time, begin thinking about how your organization, program, or service will attempt to solve the issue at hand. You will expand on each of these items in the later steps.

Outputs from this first stage should include the following:

- A problem statement describing what the issue is, who is affected, and some basic information about the causes.

- What do these individuals need to reduce the impact of their issue?

- How can your organization intervene to improve or affect this issue?

- Are there any strategies you have tried before, ruled out, or are not able to pursue due to other reasons (e.g., funding, other organizations who have a "monopoly" on that service provision)?

This process will give you the foundation or framework for the work that follows. An example of a problem statement for a fictional food bank based in Washington, DC:

The purpose of the food bank is to provide immediate and long-term support to individuals to reduce food insecurity in Washington. An estimated 66,000 people in the District are facing hunger, including 1 in 6 children. This is caused in part by the poverty rate in DC which ranks among the top 10 worst in the nation. By providing fresh, nutritious food to help immediate hunger and partnering with agencies that provide employment services we aim to reduce the impact of hunger in our community.

Stakeholder Analysis

Step 2 is the stakeholder analysis. Stakeholders are individuals who are impacted, influenced, or affected by a problem or an issue. In the first part of your stakeholder analysis, the focus should be on the individuals that you serve or will serve.

In the previous step, you developed a good understanding of the specific issue your program is aiming to affect. Now, it's important to understand the individuals that will be served. Who are they? What are their demographics? How did they come to need these services?

Your stakeholder analysis won't just involve the individuals receiving support, but it should center them. Understanding the circumstances of your clients (or potential clients if your service doesn't exist yet) is key to building a program that meets their needs.

There are a few options for how to collect this data. In some situations, distributing surveys may be an option. Online forums or communities may be a way to develop an understanding of the issues affecting your clients. At the end of the day, however, nothing replaces talking with people directly.

Although we usually talk about the primary stakeholders as the service recipients, keep in mind that they are not always clients in the traditional sense. For example, a training program to help improve educators' math teaching to their students would have those educators as the primary stakeholders, not the students.

Beyond the people that are the primary goal of the intervention, the other stakeholders are those who are affected by the program. For example, the staff who deliver the program are stakeholders, as are the funders and the wider community. Because some programs are more complex, the stakeholders can also be complex.

A crisis line that connects people to third-party counselors has those clinicians as stakeholders. The crisis workers may call 911 for an ambulance to take people to the hospital. The ambulance and the hospital they go to are also stakeholders.

The outputs from this step should include a detailed understanding of who the people your program will serve are. What criteria define them? You want to be specific. A concept in management consulting is useful here: MECE, or mutually exclusive and collectively exhaustive.

Mutually exclusive means that your stakeholders should be distinct with no overlap, and collectively exhaustive means that you should capture all the stakeholders involved.

In addition to understanding who they are, make sure you understand what the causes of their issues are. This will inform your intervention. After your stakeholder analysis, you can begin looking toward your solution in the next step.

Returning to our food bank example, the outcome of a stakeholder analysis may look like this:

- Clients of the food bank are individuals and families in the DC area who are experiencing food insecurity.

- These individuals are usually employed, though with high rents (averaging $1800 a month on a yearly pretax income of $52,000) which causes them to struggle to afford basic needs.

- Many clients of the food bank live in food deserts, where they have limited access to grocery stores and sources of less expensive food, forcing them to travel further or go without.

- Community partners assist in helping unemployed residents in the district seek employment and job training.

From this stakeholder analysis, it becomes clearer what opportunities for intervention there are. Even though the original nonprofit in our fictional example was a food bank, merely providing food may not be the best option for solving the problems of our clients.

Instead, if this were a new nonprofit, we could provide less expensive housing options and policy advocacy for reducing rents, providing support to grocery stores to open in food deserts or several other interventions beyond just providing food to hungry people, in order to ultimately reduce their dependence on the food bank.

In this way, a stakeholder analysis can help illuminate what the root causes and struggles are.

Now that the stakeholder analysis is complete, the next step is to examine the final outcome, or the way the primary stakeholders (the clients) will be when the program has achieved what it should have.

Final Outcome

The final outcome is the end goal that we want clients to experience. When forming a nonprofit and seeking 501(c)(3) tax-exempt status from the Internal Revenue Service (IRS) which is the most common tax-exempt status, you must provide a mission statement. This mission statement establishes the nonprofit was founded for a specific set of charitable aims that 501(c)(3) status sets out are allowed. For this reason, virtually every nonprofit has a mission.

The mission of the American Red Cross, for example, is:

The American National Red Cross prevents and alleviates human suffering in the face of emergencies by mobilizing the power of volunteers and the generosity of donors.

Many nonprofits also have a vision statement. While a mission statement sets out what your organization does, a vision statement sets out what the world looks like if your organization made itself obsolete. Examples include the following:

> American Diabetes Association: Life free of diabetes and all its burdens.
>
> United Way: We envision a world where every community is a resilient one, with family-sustaining jobs, good schools, and a healthy environment for all.
>
> Los Angeles Regional Foodbank: No one goes hungry in Los Angeles County.

These vision statements represent a world where that organization has fulfilled its purpose. In the same way, as you look at the final outcome of your program or service, you may also wish to write a vision statement that succinctly explains what the final outcome of that service is.

For a job placement program, the vision statement might be, "Each individual has meaningful employment, in a fulfilling organization with a living wage." For a correctional counseling program, the final goal might look like, "Clients work through their struggles and become resilient, contributing members of their communities." For a crisis line, "No person feels like suicide is their only option."

These outcomes may be achieved during the lifetime of the project, or they may be something that takes the lifetime of the client. For example, an eight-week anger management course may be the service that your organization offers, but the ultimate goal of helping someone repair their relationships with their family may take years.

This is also the opportunity for you to begin to sketch out how the final outcome is achieved through the help of others and through the complex interplay of individuals in their communities.

Returning to the example of the anger management class, this may be just one service that a person takes advantage of in their community. Although the anger management sessions equip them with the tools they need to relate more positively with those around them, the largest changes may be seen as their new confidence allows them to seek better employment, advocate for themselves more effectively, and build stronger relationships with their children. The anger management class was the stone in the pond, but the ripples extend far outward.

If your organization has multiple primary stakeholders (e.g., your program provides interrelated but distinct services to children and adults in the same family), you may have multiple final outcomes.

As an example, if a counseling program for people with substance use has adults receiving substance abuse counseling and the children receiving counseling to help them cope with a family member who is going through detox or rehab, you should expect to see somewhat different final outcomes because the circumstances that each group is dealing with are different even though they are being served by the same program and receiving broadly similar services (e.g., counseling involving substance use.) This is to be expected, especially with larger programs that involve households or families and include needs assessments to target the specific services to each person involved.

The outputs from this stage should involve impact statements of a couple of sentences, describing the final results of those individuals who have received support or experienced the intervention in your program.

Some examples of impact statements could be as follows:

- Clients no longer struggle with hunger.

- Individuals are better able to cope with the ups and downs of their life and don't see mental health as a major barrier.

- Youth formerly in prisons or jails have been released and no longer re-offend.

These are lofty goals, and that's absolutely okay! A nonprofit should set their sights high. Sometimes, setting lofty goals is what gives organizations and those that support them the energy to make real change.

Intermediate Outcomes/Outputs

Intermediate outcomes, which are also called outputs, describe the things that are measurable or observable, especially in the context of the duration of the program or service that you are providing.

For example, if you are a mental health agency that provides counseling to adults and you administer the Beck Depression Inventory to measure the level of depression in your clients during treatment, you can expect that their level of depression will decline over the course of the sessions.

It may go up at times (as examining those psychological wounds can often temporarily make people feel worse while they work through them), but if their depression is being treated effectively, we should expect to see that BDI-II score decline from the first session to the last one. This is an intermediate output, because it is one that we can measure as a direct result of the service. It may be that the goal of the counseling agency or the counseling program is to reduce depression, in which case our intermediate output is also our final outcome, but they can be different.

Another example is the food bank. While the intermediate output of providing food is an immediate and measurable reduction in hunger, the ultimate outcome of the food bank is to eliminate hunger. That can't be accomplished merely by providing people with food on an ad hoc basis. Instead, it must be achieved by attacking the roots of the issues at hand (high rents, low-paying employment, and the existence of food deserts.)

For programs already in Salesforce, one of the best sources for the data on intermediate outcomes or outputs is the data entry that the staff are doing. For example, callers to the crisis line have a conversation with a staff member who create a Case record in Salesforce Service Cloud where they provide some narrative about the situation, and they use picklists and checkboxes to select the kinds of issues the caller was dealing with, the response from the crisis worker, and the ultimate disposition or outcomes that were achieved. This data is a rich source of intermediate outcomes.

For other programs, case notes, progress notes, client notes, or many other names for this data entry performed by frontline staff may serve the same purpose. Although narrative data is not immediately usable for analysis, it provides a useful resource for this data.

When you have completed your intermediate outcomes, you should have a set of outputs that are observable from the program or service that you are delivering. There may still be some gaps in the area from the intermediate outputs and the final outcomes observed after the program ends, but all the outputs during the program should be captured.

One way to verify that your intermediate outputs are accurate is to talk to your stakeholders about them. This is a great opportunity to verify your information is accurate and to update your data collection forms to ensure you have the most accurate understanding.

Inputs and Activities

The next stage, inputs and activities, is where you document all the things that you do to achieve the outcomes that you documented earlier. If you're already delivering the program or service, this should be an easy section to complete. If you're deciding on which programs or services to offer, this section could be more time-consuming.

Understand the goal isn't to explain why the change happens. That is covered in the next section, "Change Methods." Instead, in this section, your goal is solely to document the activities themselves.

The inputs part of this section refers to the concept that activities aren't delivered in a vacuum. Inputs include the staff who deliver programs, of course, but also much more than that. For a crisis line that is volunteer-run, inputs can include the following:

- The professional staff who run the program and train volunteers

- Volunteer crisis workers who take calls

- The office space

- The telephone service

- Salesforce platform used for call-taking

As you can see, a variety of inputs go into delivering a program. It is important to understand the full spectrum of inputs because this will help illuminate your opportunities for intervening going forward.

If your organization uses Program Management Module (PMM), a part of Salesforce's Nonprofit Cloud, you may find looking at the records of the Program object and how they map onto the Service records to be illuminating.

It is also useful to understand the method of program delivery. For example, is the service delivered primarily online, in person, or a hybrid? Some programs may be different enough based on their modality that you will need separate theories of change for them.

An example of how the modality can affect the outcomes of a program is a university course that is delivered primarily through face-to-face instruction with group activities. This course may have a very different mechanism of teaching than an online, asynchronous delivery method that primarily involves self-directed reading, even if the course learning objectives and the degree issued by the university is identical.

Finally, outreach or awareness methods should be considered in this section as well. This covers all the activities that you might do to let individuals know that your service exists and to funnel them into signing up, joining the program, or otherwise being prepared to receive the program's benefits.

Awareness activities can include things like maintaining a website or social media accounts, distributing flyers to community partners, or taking out advertising in the paper or online. Outreach activities are more active and can include staffing booths at community events, having staff physically present where clients may congregate like homeless shelters, and responding to referrals received from individuals or agencies to offer your organization's supports.

The value in documenting outreach and awareness activities here is that you may find in your conversations that certain activities helped or harmed your ability to bring people into the organization, and you may need to tweak them to ensure that people have the right expectations about the issues that you can assist with and the changes they should expect.

Salesforce paid add-on tools like Marketing Cloud Account Engagement (formerly called Pardot) can be used to help you do email-based outreach, while core Salesforce features like Web-to-Lead and paid add-on unauthenticated Experience Cloud portals can help you manage inbound referrals.

Change Methods

The next task is to document the ways in which the inputs and activities noted previously influence the client. This is the "meat and potatoes" of the theory of change process and allows you to dive into the complex ways in which the interventions that you provide change the individuals and their communities to enable the outcomes that you wish to see.

Keep in mind that the ultimate changes may take years, but you should still be able to demonstrate how those final changes that you wish to see began during the intervention process.

Important components of this process include the following:

- Understanding the thoughts, feelings, and behaviors of people who have received the service or benefit.

- Documenting the learning or new skills that participants have.

- How will we know the outcome has been achieved or is being achieved?

Although your clients can give you a strong understanding of how they are helped during the service provision, several survey instruments or assessments can also be used to understand the thoughts and feelings of people who may not be the best at articulating the changes they are experiencing. An example of a tool like this is the Arizona Self Sufficiency Matrix (ASSM). With 18 domains that are each ranked on a 5-point scale, it is quick to administer and score, and you can understand changes in your clients with ease.

This is perhaps the most difficult section to do correctly because it is the one that connects the dots from the visible (the intervention and the outcome) to the invisible (all the changes that happen in between those two points.) At the same time, this stage is the most critical because it provides the internal consistency and the "glue" to the entire theory of change.

To validate your change methods are accurate, talking to your clients is valuable. You can also return to the literature review you completed in the very first step and compare the theories or explanations you may have read about to those that your clients walked you through to ensure they line up.

As the clients are the experts in their own experiences, these should be your primary source. The other material (including from the staff who deliver programs or other experts) should be a secondary source to bolster your understanding, not replace that of the client's lived experience.

In the next stage, we will take all that we have learned and begin putting it into charts, graphs, and other visuals to ensure that we have accurately captured it and simplified it enough that we can use it in material.

Sequencing and Diagramming

Sequencing and diagramming are two important tools that allow you to visualize the logic model and theory of change that you created.

Sequencing

In this stage, sequencing and diagramming, you take all that you have learned and begin visualizing it. The goal of sequencing is to begin by setting out what order each of these events should happen in. This may take more time than it looks at first glance.

For example, you have a set of activities and inputs. You have one or more final outcomes and a set of intermediate outputs that feed into those outcomes. You also have some basic understanding of who your clients are and what they look like at the beginning before your intervention or service has been delivered.

On the left are your clients, in the middle of your activities, to the right of them are the intermediate outcomes and finally on the far-right are your final outcomes.

An example of sequencing is shown in Figure 3-3, from a paper by Deborah Gate.[1]

ROOT CAUSES	NEEDS/PROBLEMS	RESOURCES/INPUTS	ACTIVITIES/OUTPUTS
In majority of cases: **Prior parenting experiences** cause absence of internal models of positive parenting due to • insufficient positive parenting or nurturance in own childhood • unresolved trauma in own childhood or adolescence • isolation or lack of parenting education and support	Parents – cognitive and emotional Low self-esteem and self-worth Low self-awareness and self-knowledge Low self-nurturance Low sense of self-efficacy and confidence in parenting Parents lack empathy for child Parents lack insight, knowledge or understanding of child's needs Parents feel isolated in own problems	Training provided centrally or locally 4 days training course led by experienced PGLTs (central) Annual refresher course (central) 2x supervisions per course (local) ?coaching and feedback? (local) Skilled PGLs/facilitators (2 per group) • Technical facilitation skills • Knowledge of parenting work –theory and best practice	Content • The 4 constructs [empathy; self-awareness; age-appropriate expectations; positive discipline] • Various exercises based on 4 constructs • Toolbox of strategies [Communication; problem-solving; negotiation; managing conflict] • Sequencing: Feelings → Behaviours → Relationships

Figure 3-3. *A Sequenced Theory of Change, licensed under CC BY 4.0*

At first glance, this seems simple. However, it's important to keep in mind that the intermediate outcomes may map onto different outcomes. For example, if one of your activities is job training, some intermediate outcomes might be realized in a matter of weeks or months as your clients begin to build additional skills.

Finding a job, however, may take much longer. And some long-term outcomes like feeling a sense of stability may take years afterward. Sequencing needs to be done carefully, so that you are appropriately matching each of the outcomes to the activities that are responsible for it.

Although you are defining a sequence, this is not set in stone. Clients are humans and they will often face setbacks and challenges, move through some stages quickly

---

[1] Ghate, D. Developing theories of change for social programmes: co-producing evidence-supported quality improvement. Palgrave Commun 4, 90 (2018). https://doi.org/10.1057/s41599-018-0139-z

and fall back to others, and so on. That's okay! We merely want to understand how a hypothetical client experience could look so that we can make sure we've backed this up based on the experiences of actual clients and the literature we've reviewed.

Diagramming

When it comes to diagramming, this involves taking the sequencing and putting it into a visual. By creating a diagram or flow chart of your theory of change, you may observe new connections or have insights that you didn't previously. You also solidify your own understanding at this point. If you can't put things onto a flow chart, you probably don't understand them as well as you may have thought you did.

A good theory of change diagram can also become a potent tool for teaching staff how your program is intended to work and may be part of a fundraising appeal or grant application as you demonstrate your organization's impact.

The diagram itself can include all the other items that we've discussed, but it can also be as simple as a logic model. In a logic model (which we discussed earlier), you diagram the situation, inputs, the activities/interventions, the outputs, and the outcomes. It is often a one-pager that provides this information at a high level. Some of the details in the complete theory of change are excluded for simplicity.

Now that you've got a complete understanding of the clients, the program you are offering them, and how they will start and finish your work with them, it is time to round out the model by looking at the external factors, the assumptions and the risks that will affect your service delivery.

External Factors

In this step, you conduct a stakeholder review and an "environmental scan." The stakeholder review involves looking at your stakeholders again, but this time focusing on the non-client stakeholders. This involves your funders, the community partners you work with, and others like the police, hospitals, or government services that intertwine to serve the same clients that you do.

Looking at your theory of change, are there things that these external stakeholders are doing to affect, either positively or negatively, your client's progress? For example, the food bank may find their work assisted by the Supplemental Nutrition Assistance Program (SNAP), also called food stamps, which provides electronic benefit transfer (EBT) cards that can be used to purchase certain eligible foods at grocery stores.

On the other hand, a restorative justice program may find that the heavy-handed approaches of the local probation and parole office interferes with their work by returning individuals to prison for minor violations even when they have come to understand the harm they have caused and their victims would prefer they remain integrated into the community.

Another part of this stage involves an environmental scan. You can use the acronym PESTEL to remember each of the aspects that comes into an environmental scan. PESTEL stands for political, economic, social, technological, environmental, and legal.

PESTEL Environmental Review

Each of the following factors can influence the environment that a nonprofit or a specific program operates in. For each of these items, consider how external factors may affect your delivery of programs or services.

Political: A health organization that provides support to transgender people may find their work more difficult if state governments make clear their policy is to not support gender-affirming care.

Economic: Widespread layoffs and a cooling of the economy place increased pressure on those living in poverty who may have less money to spend for mental health services, even when fees are token or nominal.

Social: The COVID-19 pandemic has caused some people to become more isolated and less willing to engage strangers in in-person activities.

Technological: With the widespread adoption of "smart phones," communication with clients may be easier than in the past as more people have access to an Internet-capable device or to email.

Environmental: As climate change causes changes in the weather, more and more people will find their homes unlivable after severe weather which places increased demand on a variety of support services.

Legal: Laws against feeding unhoused individuals in many states have made the work of homelessness outreach workers more difficult as they have been unable to offer this immediate assistance to hungry individuals they previously served in areas not fit for human habitation where they live.

Assumptions and Risks

Assumptions and risks are important elements of the process to ensure that you are not making basic thinking errors that will damage your analysis.

Assumptions

After completing the PESTEL analysis and stakeholder review, you are close to the end of your theory of change. The final step is to examine the assumptions and risks that underpin your analysis.

Assumptions and risks are two of the most important elements in your theory of change. Returning to the beginning of the chapter, it was Carol Weiss who noted that it was difficult to understand complex changes when the assumptions underlying those changes are unknown, unstated, or poorly supported.

For this reason, assumptions play a key role in the theory of change. Assumptions in this case are all the leaps in logic that you are making as you proceed through your theory of change.

Starting at the left-hand side of your diagram and proceeding through, where are you lacking in evidence, information, or support for the changes you want to happen? These might be areas where your program is too new to be certain what the outcomes will look like or which intermediate outputs will map to the outcomes you desire.

This might also be areas where the clients you interviewed had mentioned that they experienced these changes but couldn't be certain they were a result of your program.

Other assumptions can include that you will be able to provide the kind of service you are planning to provide, that the outcomes expected will be achieved, and so on. You should do your best to poke as many holes in your theory as possible, so that you can either collect additional supporting evidence or report these assumptions in your theory. This will ensure that you have developed the strongest theory of change you can.

Sometimes, at the assumptions stage, you will realize that your theory needs tweaking. That's okay because it is part of this process as well. Adjust the previous stages in your theory of change so that your assumptions are no longer issues.

Risks

Finally, risks are those elements that could go wrong and threaten the success of the program or the viability of the theory of change. For example, many programs assume that everyone who goes through them will experience positive impacts. Is it possible that some people who go through your program will experience negative side effects? This is a potential risk.

All programs require resources. Is this program taking resources from another program that your organization could be or should be offering? The Board may decide to redirect funding in the future, or an external major funder may stop funding this program.

Your PESTEL analysis identified a variety of external factors that may endanger the program. Any items that would pose existential risks to the existence of the program should also be mentioned here.

What happens if your program is unable to deliver the outcomes you had expected, will you face negative attention from your funders, or the wider community? These are important risks to consider so that you can have mitigation plans put in place. For example, a jobs program that sets an ambitious goal to find jobs for 10,000 people and only ends up finding jobs for 1,000 has still made a huge amount of good in their community, but that may be ignored in favor of the organization's failure to reach their ambitious stated goal.

Spend some time thinking about your assumptions and risks, and you will be better prepared to defend your theory of change.

Conclusion

Now that you've completed your theory of change, you can use it with the impact measurement and outcome evaluation frameworks that we discuss throughout the rest of this book.

Although this chapter was not as focused on Salesforce itself, this work is incredibly valuable in the work that you will do in Salesforce. For example, you can use your theory of change to build a data model for collecting the data and information that you need inside the system.

You might also update your objects and page layouts to collect information that your theory of change suggests you'll need to demonstrate the outcomes you are expecting. And you may find that you need new reports and dashboards to visualize your progress toward your goals.

In the next chapter, we will begin looking at how you can build this framework inside Salesforce and begin turning the theoretical into the practical. If you haven't been near your computer in a while, now would be a great time to boot it up and pull a Salesforce sandbox or development environment so that you can follow along as we look at how Salesforce can translate these concepts into ones you can use.

CHAPTER 4

Developing an Impact Management Strategy

In this chapter, we will look at the steps to develop an impact management strategy. First, we will start by examining your organization's strategic plan. This is the guiding document that sets out what the organization wishes to do. If you don't already have a strategic plan, now is a great time to develop one that at least covers the programs that you wish to engage in impact measurement with.

This involves figuring out what makes sense to measure, how you will collect that data, what your goals or targets are for that data, and ensuring that you have good quality data when you do collect it.

Strategic Planning

A strategic plan is a guiding document that sets out your organization's objectives. A strategic plan is usually developed by the highest level of the organization – the C-suite where one exists and identifies the direction that the organization is going. An example is shown in Figure 4-1.

© Dustin MacDonald 2023
D. MacDonald, *Impact Measurement and Outcomes Evaluation Using Salesforce for Nonprofits*,
https://doi.org/10.1007/978-1-4842-9708-7_4

Four Strategic Pillars were identified:

1. Succession Plan
2. Revenue and Sustainability
3. Membership Benefits
4. Website and Communications

In order to achieve the goals under each of these strategic pillars, the next steps will be:

1. Determine the roles and responsibilities of the Board of Directors, Executive Director and Board committees
2. Decide on the list of member benefits
3. Update the new member packet to reflect the updated list of benefits
4. Begin building each of those benefits out so that they provide the most value for members
5. Begin to assess and recruit new individual and business members

---

Figure 4-1. *A strategic plan that I assisted in*

Often, a strategic plan includes specific, measurable items or targets so that progress toward the strategic plan can be measured. More importantly, it provides insight into where leadership believes the organization should be going.

While you may not have the ability to influence your organization's strategic plan, you should absolutely get a copy of it so that you can understand where to focus your efforts. If your impact measurement is focused on areas that are misaligned with the organization's strategic plan, your efforts will not be as impactful as if you focus your efforts on building a data structure that helps illuminate the goals of the strategic plan.

Elements in a strategic plan should include the organization's current strengths and weaknesses; the mission, vision, and values of the organization; the goals for the next 3-5 years (depending on the length of the plan); and what changes need to occur for the organization to get there.

For example, if you are a mental health agency who recognizes the need to move from a practice primarily based on serving Medicaid clients to one that incorporates more private-pay clients to respond to growing expenses, your strategic plan should highlight initiatives that will help you get there.

A related concept to a strategic plan is called a balanced scorecard. This takes the strategic plan and translates it into specific measurable goals that can be monitored to understand the progress you are making toward your strategic plan. An example of a balanced scorecard from the Lucidchart software is shown in Figure 4-2.

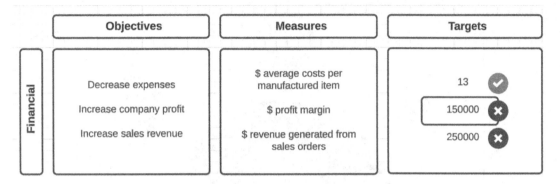

Figure 4-2. A balanced scorecard

While the strategic plan for a legal aid organization may include items like "increase our outreach to the Hispanic community who are historically underserved in our region," the balanced scorecard will include specific metrics like number of clients served, number of outreach events participated in, and number of bilingual case managers on staff. These metrics roll up to the larger strategic goal and allow everyone to understand where the organization is moving.

If your organization does not have a strategic plan, consider facilitating a session to develop one. This should include the senior leadership of the organization, but also other relevant stakeholders including staff, volunteers, and potentially even former clients who can help guide the organization. A strategic plan may be primarily text-based or graphical as shown in Figure 4-3.

Many organizations such as the United Way provide training to board members on strategic planning, and consultants can be retained relatively inexpensively to help your organization with this vital task.

Once you've written your strategic plan, it is important to refer to it regularly. A plan does no good if you put it in a drawer and never look at it again. When you go to start a new program, or evaluate an existing one, comparing it to your strategic plan is an important step to ensure you are staying on plan.

A strategic plan should be a living document that is updated regularly. It should be reviewed at least quarterly and updated yearly to adjust to changing circumstances. This ensures that it continues to be a useful document for guiding the strategic future of the organization.

Too often, organizations focus on the money coming in and forget to check that against their strategic priorities. An unfocused organization will be less effective than one that carefully chooses where to place resources and assets.

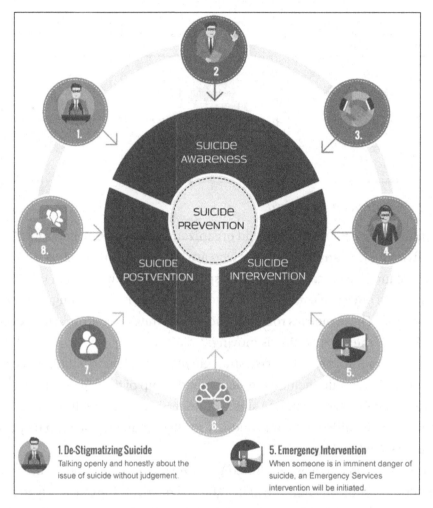

Figure 4-3. *Shows an example of a graphics-based strategic plans*

Selecting Indicators and Metrics

Before you can begin to do any impact measurement or outcome evaluation, you need to decide what is important to the organization. Your strategic plan should be the first source of indicators and metrics; it is by no means the only place to find this information.

Each department in an organization likely has its own internal goals that are important to meeting whichever priorities they have. These can be tangible goals like serving a certain number of clients or more intangible things like increasing awareness of a program or building stronger relationships with the community.

Understanding what motivates each department will be important in selecting indicators and metrics that are useful to that department. Interviews can be helpful in this regard: by asking the department head what they want to track, what they struggle to track right now, and what is the most important thing for them to understand from their data, you will likely find that the right metrics and indicators naturally "bubble up" to the surface.

Once you've identified the metrics and indicators, you need to assess whether you have that data in your system. It's likely that you have at least some of these important items being tracked, but it's possible that they are not stored in the most effective way. For example, if attendance at group counseling sessions is important but you currently track that through narrative case notes, you can't quickly tell who has attended a session or not.

Often, you'll find that the information exists in some form but it's far from ideal. This is where assessing the data model becomes important. By thinking about the best way to store information, you can improve the data collection and management process.

If you find yourself having difficulty selecting metrics, a few tips can be helpful. Start with what you already track, if you track anything. Are these metrics relevant to the program? For example, tracking the number of clients that a counseling program serves may be useful, but if you don't know whether the clients who are being served are getting better or not, it may not be the most effective indicator.

Indicators should be based on what is important in the program, not just what data you currently have. The most effective indicator may be one from a pre- and posttest, even if you are not currently administering one.

As mentioned earlier in this book, you should ensure that your goals and metrics are SMART: specific, measurable, achievable, realistic, and timely. This will allow them to be monitored. If they are too vague to be monitored, you won't know if you are making progress toward them.

Collecting and Managing Data

Assessing all the data points that you want to collect is important. Once you understand where all the data you are looking for lives, and how much of it is not being collected at all, you are ready to begin to improve the data collection process.

Creating a spreadsheet or chart to list each of these data points can be helpful. You can include what the data point is, where in the system it is stored, or in what format it is captured (e.g., text, picklist, checkbox). Once you've identified the gaps, you can plan for how you will fill in that data.

If you have not used it before, Salesforce's Schema Builder can also be a useful reference here. Schema Builder allows you to see every Object in your Salesforce organization and the fields that go with. You can also easily add fields to fill out the data model as needed. A screenshot of Schema Builder is shown in Figure 4-4.

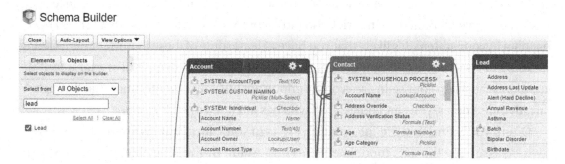

Figure 4-4. *Schema Builder showing the account, contact, and lead objects*

In most cases, text data is difficult or impossible to analyze in a reliable way. Although there are qualitative analysis techniques such as thematic analysis where you "code" extracts of text with relevant keywords, the amount of effort required to do so is often cost and time prohibitive.

Instead, you should utilize picklists, checkboxes, radio buttons, and other ways of collecting data that ensure that you can easily analyze the data without needing to extract it, manually process it, and then determine the content.

Salesforce makes it easy to get data into the system by ensuring that all data entry into the system is automatically stored in the database in the form of objects and fields; however, once they are in the system, you need to be able to get the information out when it is relevant. This is where reports, dashboards, list views, and other Salesforce features and functionality can come in handy.

If you have data in external systems, you can also get this data into Salesforce. There are a few methods to accomplish this. One is by direct Salesforce integration. The other is by importing data using a tool inside Salesforce like Import Wizard, Salesforce Data Loader (which is a downloaded application), or a third-party website like `https://dataloader.io`. You can see a screenshot of Data Loader in Figure 4-5.

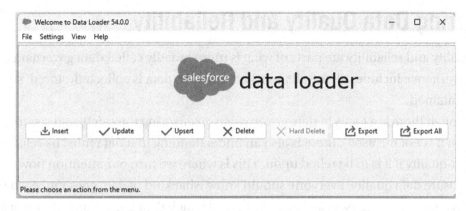

Figure 4-5. *Salesforce Data Loader*

Once you've addressed all your missing data points, you are ready to set targets and baselines for the goals that you've identified.

Establishing Baselines and Targets

Baselines and targets are two important elements of developing your impact management strategy. A baseline, as the name suggests, is wherever that goal or metric is now. You can't improve on something unless you understand where you are right now.

Salesforce Reports can be a valuable source of baseline data by allowing you to understand what your metrics look like this year or this quarter.

Once you understand the baseline, you can begin to set new targets that represent your goal. Returning to your strategic plan or balanced scorecard, ensure that you have mapped each of your strategic plan items to your scorecard.

If you don't have a good sense of your targets, there are a few ways to figure them out. One is to touch base with other organizations that work in the same "industry" that you do. For example, a legal aid organization in Pennsylvania may reach out to a similar organization in nearby New York to find out what their targets look like. In this way, benchmarking can help you decide on what a realistic number looks like – keeping in mind that different populations, different situations, and different operating environments can cause the targets to need to be adjusted a bit.

The other way you can choose a target is simply to improve on your baseline. If you set a goal of 10 or 20% more intakes next year compared to this year, you can get a sense of what should increase.

Ensuring Data Quality and Reliability

Data quality and reliability are parts of what is more broadly called data governance. Data governance includes all the elements around how data is collected, stored, shared, and maintained.

Although there is a focus in data governance on ensuring the safety and security of data (that it is not misused), there is also an understanding that data must be reliable and high-quality if it is to be relied upon. This is where we turn our attention now.

To ensure data quality, everyone should know what kind of data goes into each field in your Salesforce org. If users are confused about which data goes where, they will be unable to ensure they enter data in the right place.

Another important element of data quality is ensuring users cannot enter obviously false information. For example, if you have a Program Engagement with a start date of June 1, you should not be able to put an End Date of May 1. Obviously, a client should not end their time in a program a month before they started it. The way to prevent this kind of obvious data entry error is with Salesforce Validation Rules, an example of which is shown in Figure 4-6.

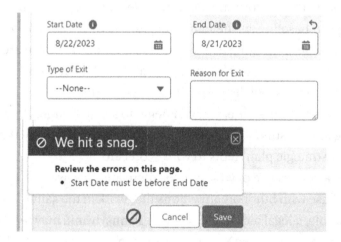

Figure 4-6. *An example of a validation rule from the Salesforce Trailhead on creating validation rules*

Validation rules allow you to use formula logic so that only when the conditions of the formula are met (such as the Program Engagement Start Date being earlier than the Program Engagement End Date) can you save the record.

For more information on Validation Rules, see Chapter 5 or the Trailhead Module on Creating Validation Rules which you can find at `https://trailhead.salesforce.com/content/learn/modules/point_click_business_logic/validation_rules`.

Conclusion

In this chapter, we reviewed how to develop an impact management strategy by completing a strategic plan, selecting indicators and metrics, collecting data, and reviewing your progress toward the target. In the next chapter, we'll look at how we go from the theoretical strategy to building it inside Salesforce.

CHAPTER 5

Creating the Framework in Salesforce

Now that you've created a theory of change, you are ready to begin using Salesforce to build out this theory of change. If you are already using Salesforce, you likely already have a data model in place. If this is a new program, however, you will need to do some prep work.

As a business analyst, you will need to understand how to translate nonprofit program requirements into Salesforce features and functions so that you can ask questions with sufficient detail that you can understand what the agency needs.

As an architect, you'll want to understand how to translate the theory of change into an effective data model that takes advantage of Salesforce functionality and is both user-friendly and scalable.

For nonprofit program managers or measurement and evaluation (M&E) staff, this chapter will help you understand how you'll use Salesforce to accomplish your day-to-day tasks of reporting, visualizing data, and ensuring clean data input so that you can rely on the information your staff are putting into the system.

In the previous chapter, we focused on data for strategy, but here are much more focused on the data used in the day-to-day delivery of your programs and measuring the impact and outcomes of that service delivery.

Creating (or Documenting) Your Data Model

For this chapter, we'll assume that you have not used Salesforce before and are building out your data model for the first time. Obviously if you do have an existing data model, you'll be more limited in how you can change it, but "refactoring" is definitely a common practice, and you may come away from this chapter with some additional ideas about how to improve things.

© Dustin MacDonald 2023
D. MacDonald, *Impact Measurement and Outcomes Evaluation Using Salesforce for Nonprofits*,
https://doi.org/10.1007/978-1-4842-9708-7_5

In Salesforce, each set of data (such as information about a person, a task, or a household) is stored in an Object. These objects have descriptive names like Contact, Task, or Account. Salesforce includes a variety of standard objects for each of its versions. Sales Cloud contains objects to track sales pipelines; Service Cloud contains objects to track customer service.

Some of the most important standard objects include the following:

- Account

- Case

- Contact

- Lead

- Opportunity

- Task

Each of these objects contains fields that store the data in the object. Knowing both which objects you are using and the fields is critical to building or maintaining your data model. This is because when you go to make updates, you want to make sure that you are not duplicating fields across different objects or creating new objects that replace what you have already created.

Object Manager, one of the ways to maintain your objects and fields is shown in Figure 5-1. Another is Schema Builder, covered in the previous chapter.

Figure 5-1. *Some of the fields on the Account object in Salesforce*

Additionally, the type of field is relevant as well. You might think that you have the data that you need, but it is stored in the form of text fields, where what you really want to report out on is a picklist or drop-down. Similarly, you might think that a picklist is exactly what you need for a certain use case, but if it is missing the answers you were expecting, your ability to report out on it will be more limited than if it were an open text field.

As a business analyst, measurement and evaluation (M&E) staff member or other person with responsibility for data governance – that is, ensuring clean, reliable data is available to the organization, becoming an expert on your organization's data model – is critical to success.

When you add Nonprofit Cloud Case Management (NCCM) or Program Management Module (PMM), you'll have additional objects added. For example, PMM includes the objects Program and Service. Custom objects, including the custom objects that come along with NCCM and PMM, have a suffix of __c for custom. This means that while the label is Program, the name used in the back end of the system is Program__c. NCCM also has a variety of custom objects like those for tracking Case Plans, Intakes, and an advanced version of Client Notes.

All objects and fields in Salesforce have both a human-readable label and an API name used by the system in the background.

Salesforce provides an Entity Relationship Diagram or ERD for both NCCM and PMM, so you can understand the relationships between the different objects. You can see the ERD depicted in Figure 5-2. Under each object is a set of fields, or places for data input.

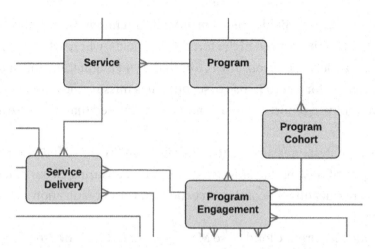

Figure 5-2. *A segment of an Entity Relationship Diagram produced by Salesforce for the NCCM/PMM program showing the relationship between different objects[1]*

For example, the Assessment object includes fields to track the Assessment Name, the Client Name who is receiving or completing the assessment, and the Assessment Completed Date. You also have the option to add to these custom fields.

Chances are good that while you can create fields on standard objects for the majority of your needs, you will find yourself needing additional custom objects for your unique needs.

In order to determine which custom objects you'll need, you can start by doing an audit of all of the documentation that you require clients to fill out as part of the intake, assessments, and service delivery and all of the documentation that staff complete like progress notes, needs assessments, and so on. Map each piece of data to an object and a field.

You might find that certain objects are unique enough that they don't really fit within any of the objects that you have. For example, let's say that your organization has volunteers who need to complete background checks. You could track that information under the Contact object, but maybe they'll complete multiple background checks during their time with the organization, and you want to be able to track how those results have changed over time.

---

[1] This ERD can be accessed at the URL https://help.salesforce.com/s/articleView?id=sfdo. CM_ERD.htm&type=5.

Assessment could work for background checks, but maybe you want only certain users to be able to access this background check data, while everyone can access the Assessment object. In this case, a custom object might make sense.

When you create a custom object, you'll give it both a human-readable name or label (like Background Checks) and an API or internal system name (Background_Checks__c) and then create a set of fields on it. When those fields link to other objects (such as a field called Client which points to the Contact who the background check involves), those fields are called lookup relationships. These will be represented on the ERD and be a fundamental part of the glue that binds your data model together.

There are other kinds of relationships such as Master-Detail Relationships that enable special functionality like rollup summaries to count the number of times a child record exists and display it on the parent object, but for now understand that you'll need to know how each object connects to the other objects in your data model.

Remember MECE? Mutually exclusive and collectively exhaustive. This is another situation for the MECE principle.

You don't want too many custom objects, because it can be confusing for end users to know where data is located (and because Salesforce provides limits on the number you can have) but also because a simpler data model is easier to maintain.

Once you know what kind of Custom Objects you need, and the fields that will accompany them, you are ready to begin creating and connecting them. When you have finished this process, you will have a solid data model.

Example Data Model

A legal aid society has decided to stand up Salesforce. They have NCCM and PMM. Looking at their objects, they decide to use the following standard and custom objects from NCCM and PMM:

- Lead: A person who has expressed interest in legal support but has not yet completed an intake

- Account: Represents the household of a client, and also organizations

- Contact: Someone the organization is actively working with

- Case: Used for referrals

- Intake: For collecting initial information about new clients

- Program: Stores information on the legal programs the organization offers

- Program Engagement: A specific individual enrollment in a program

- Assessment: Used during the intake to collect information on the client's legal aid needs

- Service: Stores information on the services the organization offers which are tied to the various legal programs

- Service Delivery: Represents specific client meetings or other services delivered to clients

- Service Schedule: A schedule of services that will be offered at specific dates/times. In this case, group sessions on various legal issues like immigration

- Service Session: A specific session (e.g., the January 5 group session)

- Service Participant: A Contact who will be attending a specific Service Session

After evaluating the objects they have available, the organization decides to create some custom objects to track information specific to their needs:

- Legal Issue: An object for recording the information on the specific criminal offense or legal issue that each client is dealing with

- Expungements: An object for tracking the status of expungements which have their own processes separate from other legal issues

- Volunteers: An object for recording the details of the organization's volunteers

- Background Checks: An object for tracking the background check details of volunteers

These custom objects exist alongside the others and allow the organization to track all of the information that it needs for day-to-day operations. Having a quality data model is an important part of data hygiene, which means to have high-quality, complete, accurate data in your organization.

Data Model and Your Theory of Change

One way to ensure that your data model is accurate is to look at your theory of change. Are all of the elements that you identified in the theory of change represented somewhere? For example, you should have objects that allow you to track each of the outputs and outcomes that you identified. If you don't have a spot to store the data you need, you'll be unable to leverage the full power of the theory of change you've created.

Creating reports

Once you've figured out your data model and created the custom objects that you will need, it's time to consider what kind of reporting you will need to do. No matter your role in the organization, you likely have someone who is monitoring the activity of the organization for different purposes.

As an executive director, you may need to provide data to your board of directors for them to exercise their oversight capability, to funders, and to community partners or the media. As a program manager, you may report to your direct supervisor or the executive director but also ad hoc requests that may go to other departments or the media.

As a frontline staff member, you may be creating reports to help you do better case management by identifying individuals who are overdue for appointments or finding clients with missing data. If you are responsible for exporting data to other platforms like a financial system, you may also use reports to accomplish this.

An excerpt of an example report is shown in Figure 5-3.

Report: Contacts & Accounts
Client Records Missing Phone Number
How many Client records are missing phone numbers? (Used on PMM Home Page)

Total Records
19

Mailing Country ↑	Contact ID	First Name	Last Name ↑	Email	Phone
- (11)	0038I00000KUPmm	Jodi	Anderson	-	☎ -
	0038I000007n2Xp	Robinson	Crusoe	-	☎ -
	0038I000007n7Gs	Merv	Griffin	dustin.macdonald@provisiopartners.com	☎ -
	0038I00000AUf4p	Bojack	Horseman	-	☎ -
	0038I000007HIQE	John	Jobseeker	-	☎ -

Figure 5-3. *A sample report from PMM*

When you create a report, you will have access to all of the fields included in your selected report type. These fields can be added to the report as columns.

Report Types

In Salesforce, when you go to create a report, the first thing you are prompted for is to select the report type. A report type contains a primary object and up to three related objects, with each of the related objects either being mandatory or optional.

For example, you could have a report type of Accounts and Contacts where each Account that appears could have related Contacts. In this case, you would see Accounts with no Contacts associated with them. Instead, if you selected the Accounts with Contacts report type, you will only see Accounts that also have associated Contact records.

There are two kinds of report types, standard and custom. Standard is exactly what it sounds like: the report types that come out of the box with Salesforce, for example, Campaigns with Contacts.

Custom Report Types

If you're doing anything complex at all, or building any reports with custom objects - which is likely - you'll need to use Custom Report Types. Custom Report Types work exactly the same as standard ones except that you can define the objects and whether the related objects are required or optional.

When you go to add new custom reports, you'll be asked to select the objects that they apply to with a handy graphic to help you ensure you are selecting the right objects for the use case you are solving (see Figure 5-4).

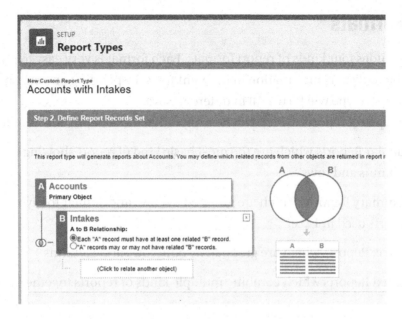

Figure 5-4. *A Custom Report Type being created*

You can see Report Types, both custom and standard, by going to Setup and typing Report Types. You'll find it under the clickpath Features Settings ➤ Analytics ➤ Reports & Dashboards ➤ Report Types. Figure 5-5 shows several custom report types used with Salesforce Field Service.

Edit | Del	Voice Calls	Voice Calls
Edit | Del	Voice Calls with Cases	Voice Calls with Cases
Edit | Del	Voice Calls, Case, WO, SA	Voice Calls With Cases and Work Orders and Service Appointments
Edit | Del	Work Orders and SA	Work Orders with Service Appointments
Edit | Del	Work Orders with Service Appointments	Work Orders with Service Appointments report

Figure 5-5. *Several custom report types*

Here is an example of some custom report types in an organization that takes calls and dispatches individuals using Salesforce Field Service. The objects involved in this work include Voice Calls to take phone calls, Work Orders to decide what work needs to be done, and Service Appointments for the date, time, and specific person who will be responding.

Report Formats

Salesforce includes four kinds of report formats. Each format is very easy to put together but allows you to display information in different ways. Depending on your specific needs, each report type will be useful in different ways.

The four types of reports, which will be explored in more depth, are as follows:

- Tabular Reports which are the most basic kind of report showing columns and rows

- Summary Reports, which are grouped by rows and similar to pivot reports used in Excel

- Matrix Reports which are grouped by both rows and columns

- Joined Reports which combine multiple kinds of reports together

Fields

Before discussing the different kinds of reports, it makes sense to talk about fields. Fields represent the columns that exist on your object. All of the columns will be represented as text. For example, a last name will display as the text in that field, while a picklist will show the value selected for that picklist.

Multi-select picklists are challenging. These fields allow multiple values to be selected. For example, if you have a Region__c picklist that allows you to select which regions a client receives services in, you might select "North" and "East." On the report, this will be displayed as "North; East."

Figure 5-6 shows an example of a multi-select picklist from the Volunteers for Salesforce (V4S) package, used to select which skills a potential volunteer has.

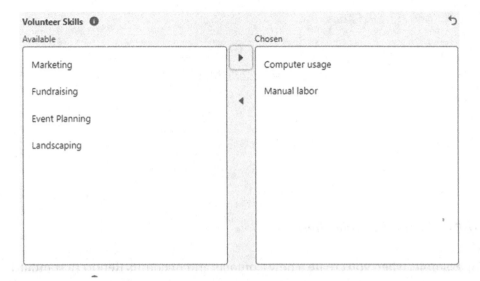

Figure 5-6. *A multi-select picklist. The background is yellow because the record is being edited*

Multi-select picklists are challenging to report on, because if you try to filter by Region EQUALS North, the value "North; East" will not be shown. Instead, you need to use Region CONTAINS North, which will then show you both "North" and "North; East."

Filters

After choosing your report type and deciding on the fields that will be necessary as columns on your report, the next thing to determine are the filters you will need. All reports have some kind of filter, because Salesforce chooses a couple of default filters when you open the report. An example of some filters are included in Figure 5-7.

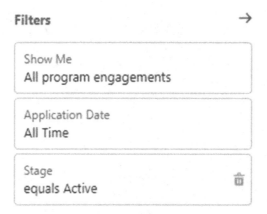

Figure 5-7. *Some example filters*

For example, when you create a new Contacts and Accounts Report (a standard report), you'll be presented with filters to show you whose reports (with the options being "My contact," "My accounts," "My team's accounts," and "All accounts") and the Created Date field.

The majority of reports will require some more complex filters than the defaults, but luckily Salesforce gives you lots of options. For text fields, your options include the following:

- Equals

- Not equal to

- Less than

- Greater than

- Less or equal

- Greater or equal

- Contains

- Does not contain

- Starts with

Currency and numerical fields have very similar filter options as text fields, as do a variety of less common data types like Addresses, Phone Numbers, and Email Address (which, behind the scenes, are often stored as text as well).

For Currency fields in particular, you can also combine them with a field comparison. So you could have a report that shows you the value of a donor's Largest Gift when it is equal to their Last Donation (another field on the same object), meaning their most recent gift was at least the same size as their last donation, if not the same gift.

For date fields, you can choose a variety of standard options like Current Fiscal Year (FY), Previous Calendar Year (CY), Last Week, Last Month, or exact date ranges. Salesforce supports both relative and defined dates, so you can say "Last 40 Days" or "Next 100 Days" (for due dates in the future).

Cross Filters

One more advanced element of Salesforce reports is cross filters, shown in Figure 5-8. These allow you to filter across related objects. For example, returning to our Accounts and Contacts report example, you might be a fundraiser staff person who wants to see all of the Contacts attached to Accounts where the Account Type equals Foundation.

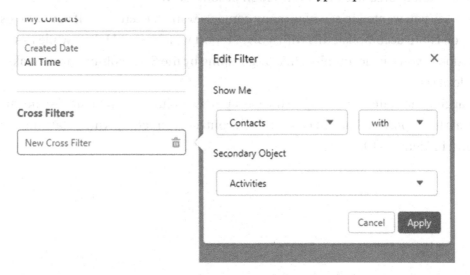

Figure 5-8. *A cross filter to show all Contacts that have accompanying activities like Tasks or Events*

Without cross filters, you would need to create a Formula Field on the Contact that stores the associated Account's Account Type. If this is a one-off request, you might not want to clutter up your Contact object with this additional field. Instead, by using a cross filter you can pull this information with just a few clicks.

Tabular Reports

A tabular report is the most basic form of report. When you create a report, you will have the ability to add each of the fields to the report as columns and display the records as rows. For example, on Contact you have access to First Name, Last Name, Title, Birthdate, Account Name, and so on.

By adding filters you can ensure that you only see the columns that you need to see. When you are ready, you can also export this report, and the others following. Your options for exporting include a basic CSV/XLSX report format or a formatted report that preserves the appearance of the report on the screen and is more useful for printing.

Summary Report (Grouped by Rows)

Let's say you have a Contacts and Accounts Report and you've set the filters to show you all Contacts, created all time. Right now you're seeing every contact in your organization. You likely want to organize this information in some way.

Let's say you wanted to see how many contacts were in each state. If you were using Excel, you could accomplish this with a pivot report which would take a while to set up. In Salesforce, you can accomplish this by grouping by the State column, which takes just a couple of seconds.

Dragging the State column up to the Group Rows column as in Figure 5-9 instantly reformats the report so that you can see each contact grouped by which state they're in, as shown in Figure 5-10.

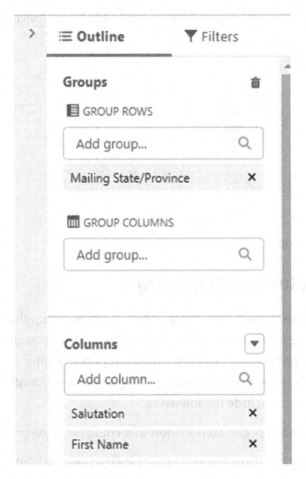

Figure 5-9. *Grouping by Mailing State*

At the bottom of the report, you'll see the Row Counts controls at the bottom of the screen. By toggling the Detail Rows, the individual entries will disappear and be replaced with a count of each state and how many records match.

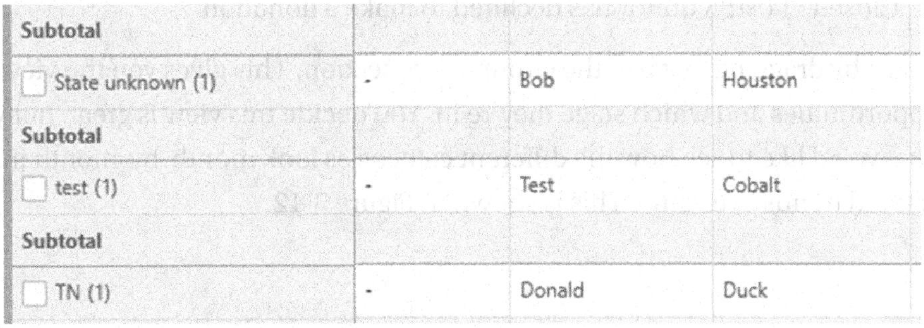

Subtotal			
State unknown (1)	-	Bob	Houston
Subtotal			
test (1)	-	Test	Cobalt
Subtotal			
TN (1)	-	Donald	Duck

Figure 5-10. *The result of grouping by state*

Another advantage of grouping is that you can add charts to visualize the data. Some available charts are shown in Figure 5-11.

Figure 5-11. *Chart options*

Matrix Report (Rows and Columns)

Matrix reports are an extension from the grouping by rows option that make up the summary report. When you group by both rows and columns, you gain the ability to do more complex visualizations. You can see a matrix report in Figure 5-13.

For example, let's say you want to see your Opportunities (donations) in Salesforce by stage. Example stages include the following:

- Identification: A potential donation that could be received.

- Qualification: You are assessing how much a potential donor may be able to contribute.

- Prospecting: You are actively in communication, pursuing a donor for a donation.

- Closed - Won: A donor has made a donation!

- Closed - Lost: A donor has declined to make a donation

You start by dragging Stage to the Group Rows section. This gives you the view of all the opportunities and which stage they're in. You decide this view is great, but you decide that you'd like to see how the different categories look month-by-month in order to understand trends over time. This is shown in Figure 5-12.

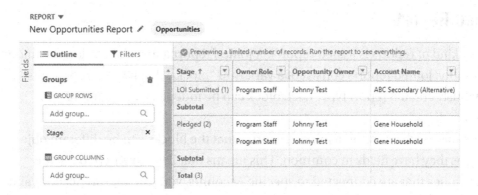

Figure 5-12. *An Opportunity Report grouped by Stage*

In order to achieve this, you first drag Close Date to the Group Column section. This gives you the stages as rows, with each day being represented as a column. In order to transform the view to see by month (summing the days), you can click the arrow beside Close Date, scroll down to "Group Date By...," and select Calendar Month.

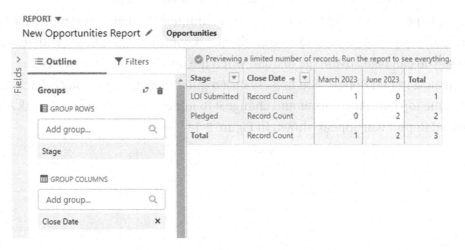

Figure 5-13. *A completed Matrix Report*

Now your matrix report allows you to see how opportunity stages change each month. You can use matrix reports for a variety of complex visualizations.

Joined Reports

The last kind of reports is joined reports. A joined report allows for the largest amount of flexibility. Joined reports consist of a variety of "blocks." Each block represents a previously created report type. Each block can be independently filtered and customized.

The major advantage to a joined report is that the blocks can be different objects, as long as they have fields in common. This means that if you wanted to see the opportunities that are connected to specific Accounts, you can take an Account and Contacts report and join it with an Opportunity report.

By grouping the Account Name across blocks, you can now see the Opportunities attached to each Account. You might ask yourself: how is that different from just using a standard Opportunity? In a joined report, you have access to all of the columns from both report types. So while in a standard Opportunity grouped by Account Name you only have access to the Opportunity columns, here you can continue to filter and display all of the fields available on the Account and the Opportunity object!

Joined Reports are one of the most useful techniques for seeing complex data, but it can take a bit to wrap your head around them. I recommend practicing with joined reports so you can take advantage of them when the opportunity presents itself.

To create a Joined Report, you first create a regular report. Then, you click the Report button in the top left-hand corner and change it to Joined Report. Once you click Apply, your Joined Report will appear, shown in Figure 5-14.

Figure 5-14. *Choosing a Joined Report*

This new Joined Report has no blocks yet, just the report that we originally turned into a Joined Report (in this case, Contacts and Accounts.) We're going to join this report with our Opportunity report from earlier in order to see it in action. We do that by clicking the Add Block button and then choosing Opportunity on the Report Type screen, shown in Figure 5-15.

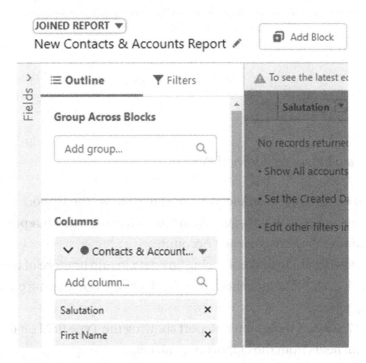

Figure 5-15. *A new Joined Report*

We now have two blocks, visible in Figure 5-16. I've clicked the arrow beside them to collapse them so I can show you them both at once. You can rename these blocks if needed, so you can keep track in more complex reports.

Figure 5-16. *Two blocks in a Joined Report*

Returning to our original example of a report that shows the Opportunities across the Accounts, you can group by the Account Name (which exists in both reports) in order to see the Opportunities that exist on each Account.

If you are following along and not seeing any data in one or more of the blocks, make sure you also click each block and check that the filters are not filtering out the data you're expecting to see.

In Figure 5-17, we can see a Joined Report showing the Type field on the Account object and several fields from the Opportunity object.

Figure 5-17. *Our completed Joined Report*

Subscribe to Reports

Another feature that you should be aware of is the ability to schedule or subscribe to reports. This feature is called *Scheduling* in Salesforce Classic, the older version/view of Salesforce, and *Subscribe* in Lightning Experience (the modern version; see Figure 5-18).

Figure 5-18. *The Subscribe option in Salesforce Lightning Experience*

When you click the Subscribe button, you are prompted to select how often you want to receive reports as in Figure 5-19. This can be Daily, Weekly, or Monthly. For each frequency, you're given options to fine-tune exactly when you want to receive the report, such as 7 a.m. if daily, Monday and Wednesday if weekly, or the Fourth Tuesday in the month if monthly.

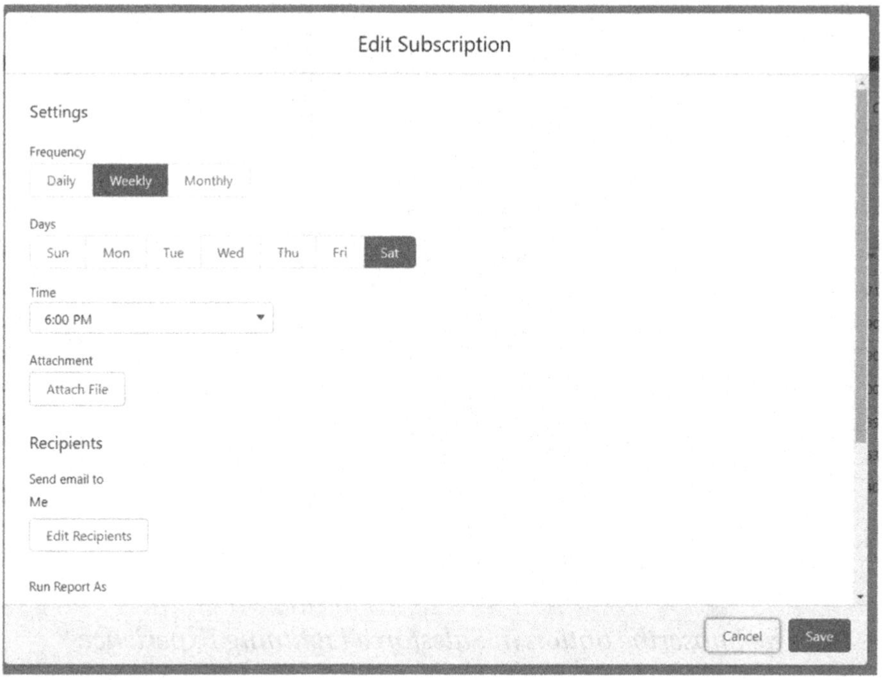

Figure 5-19. *The Subscription options*

Recipients and Running User

Once you've selected the frequency, you next select the recipients. This will default to yourself but you can add other users. You can define who the report should run as: yourself or another user.

Running as another user is useful for situations when the report is set up to show the results of the running user, but you want to send that report to someone else.

For example, a case manager's Caseload report is set up to show "My Program Engagements." If the case manager's supervisor opens this report or subscribes to it without customization, it will show the supervisor's program engagements, which is obviously not what we want. By changing the running user to indicate the case manager, the program manager can subscribe to it and see the correct results.

Conditions

One of the most useful components of subscribing to reports is the conditions section. This allows you to set a variety of conditions that will trigger the export to happen. With no conditions, the report fires at the designated time each week. If you set conditions, the report will only send when those conditions are met.

Conditions can include both field values and record count. An example of filtering on field value is a report about overdue bills that shouldn't be emailed to Finance until the amount is over $1000.

An example of using a record count is a report that shows when required fields are missing that only fires when the record count is equal to or greater than 1. With this condition set, you will only get notified of missing data when there actually are records to correct. With conditions, you can "set it and forget it," rather than needing to repeatedly revisit a report to find out if there are items to take action on.

This is shown in Figure 5-20.

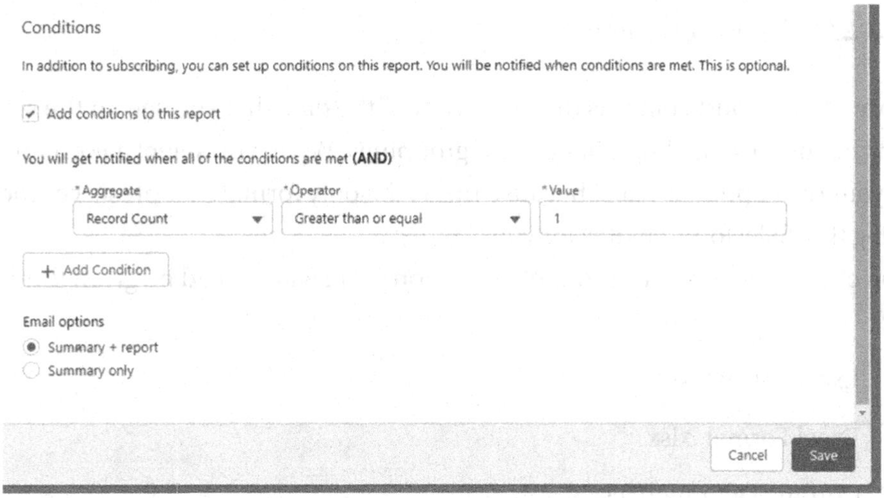

Figure 5-20. *Conditions in Salesforce Reports*

Export Reports

Exporting reports was briefly discussed earlier. This functionality allows you to take a copy of the report you have produced and export it or embed into another program like a Word document or PowerPoint presentation or for further analysis.

When you go to export a report, you are presented with two options, shown in Figure 5-21. The first is a Formatted Report.

Figure 5-21. *Exporting a report*

A Formatted Report contains the exact view of the data that you see on the screen, including details like headings, filters, and groupings. When you select a Formatted Report, your only option is Excel because this is the only format that preserves the formatting that Salesforce creates for you.

If you choose Details Only (your other option), you will instead be given three options:

- Excel Format .xls

- Excel Format .xlsx

- Comma Delimited .csv

For the XLS and CSV formats, you can also choose the text encoding. These detail exports include only the rows and columns from the report (with filters applied), but none of the other formatting. This makes them ideal for additional analysis, producing visualizations in Excel or Tableau, and for importing into other programs.

Einstein Discovery for Reports

Einstein Discovery for Reports (EDR) is an interesting paid add-on to reports that puts an Analyze button at the top of your reports. When you click it, EDR gets to work and produces regression analyses for each of the columns in the report. This allows you to then look at the correlations that result from each of the columns, to understand how the columns affect each other.

Once this is complete, you can ask EDR to show you correlations that help you achieve specific outcomes. For example, if you look at an Opportunities report and you want to know what statistically significant results correlate with an opportunity stage of "Closed - Converted," EDR can examine your opportunities and provide you with this insight.

While it's a very useful tool and embedded right inside Salesforce, you can also complete this sort of analysis using R or a third-party tool (even Excel if you are careful enough), and therefore you may not need this particular paid product to meet your needs. If you are already using Tableau CRMA, however, you likely have access to Einstein Discovery for Reports, and so it may make sense to use it.

Creating Dashboards

We've discussed a lot about reports, but those are only half of the capability that Salesforce provides you to visualize data. The other option is a dashboard. Dashboards allow you to take reports and place them on a canvas. By doing so, you gain access to some additional functionality.

A screenshot of a dashboard that comes with NCCM is shown in Figure 5-22. Each dashboard component is sourced from a different report, which is shown at the bottom of each tile on the dashboard.

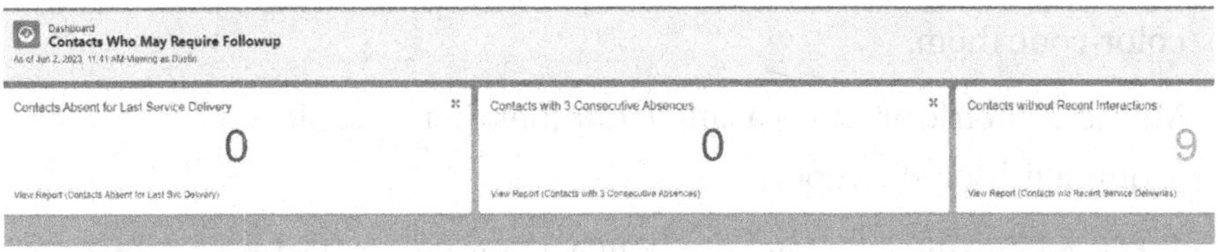

Figure 5-22. *A dashboard*

First, dashboards can display the data from many reports. Unlike reports, you're not limited to a single report type or even related reports or fields like in Joined Reports. You can display totally unrelated reports on the same dashboard.

Second, dashboards allow you to display data as a different running user. Similar to a subscribed report, you can display a dashboard as yourself, but also as a specific running user who has different data access than yourself. This can allow you to create a dashboard based on high-level data in the organization but share a summary version of it with people lower down who need the high-level insights but not the ability to drill into the detailed report data.

The Dashboard Editor is shown in Figure 5-23. This is where you drag the tiles onto the dashboard canvas.

Figure 5-23. *The Dashboard being edited*

Finally, dashboards contain a wide variety of components that are not present on reports. Examples of these components include the following:

- Chart: A chart is a visual representation of data in the form of a bar chart, pie chart, scatterplot, or several other options.

- Gauge: A gauge allows you to show your progress toward a specific number. You can highlight the low, medium, and high values and color-code them.

- Metric: A metric or KPI is a single number that is displayed prominently on the report.

- Table: A table displays very much like a report on a dashboard, in a tabular format.

- Custom components: If you have coding skills, you can build Visualforce pages that extend the capabilities of your dashboards.

These components are shown in Figure 5-24.

Figure 5-24. *Several of the component options available for dashboards*

Dashboard Filters

One of the most powerful elements of a dashboard is the ability to apply a dashboard filter. Unlike a report filter which exists in the background and isn't obvious when viewing a report, dashboard filters are visible right on the dashboard and can be adjusted by the person viewing the dashboard.

Because you have multiple reports on the dashboard, your filter can affect all of them. This means if you had a set of reports showing you a variety of demographics about clients, you could add a Created Date filter and give it values of "Last 30 Days," "Last 60 Days," and "Last 12 Months."

When you select the dashboard filter, all of the reports on the dashboard filter their data to match the chosen filter, without you needing to create new reports that have the specified filters. In a few seconds, you're seeing the filtered version of the data. Even better, when you return to this dashboard again, the filter you selected will remain until you change it to a different one. This makes dashboards a useful tool for providing oversight and quickly sorting through data to find the insights you need.

Reports and dashboards are both valuable ways of displaying data, but sometimes the data you need isn't available on the objects yet. Turning to formulas and validation rules next, we ensure we have the right data in the right places.

Using Formulas and Validation Rules

Formulas and validation rules are two powerful weapons in an arsenal of Salesforce tools to ensure good data hygiene. Formulas allow you to perform custom calculations on records and related records and use them in formulas, validation rules (see next), list views, and other places you would store data.

Formula Fields

First we need to look at formulas that you might encounter or create on an object. Functions are created by applying a variety of functions on a formula field. When you create a new field on an object, you can choose Formula as a data type. Next, you are prompted for the formula output type. Formulas can return text, date, numbers, and several other formats. This is important because if you try to return text to a formula that was expecting a date, for example, you will get an error.

Once you've selected your return type, you are brought to the formula builder. Here you will write the syntax of the formula.

Salesforce provides a number of functions or commands you can use in the formula. Basic functions include things like + for addition and - for subtraction but also more complex items like IF statements that let you evaluate a set of conditions and return different values depending on the criteria; logical operators like AND, OR, and less than/ greater than; and more.

Basic Examples

Length of Service

A case management program provides 90 days of counseling starting from the first day the program engagement was created. Case managers want to know how many days they have remaining in their 90 days. The formula field called Days_Until_Expiry__c is created, with a return type of Date.

The formula becomes (CreatedDate + 90) - TODAY().

This formula takes the date the Program Engagement was created (for simplicity, we can say January 1) and then adds 90 days to figure out the last day they will be eligible for counseling. By subtracting that day (April 1) from today's date (let's say February 21), we arrive at 39 days remaining.

Scoring Assessments

Another example involves an assessment. This assessment is a short version of the Arizona Self-Sufficiency Matrix that includes five picklists. Each of the picklists refers to a different domain: housing, employment, life skills, mental health, and safety.

Each of the picklists is rated on a scale from 1 to 5, where 1 is no self-sufficiency or safety and 5 is complete self-sufficiency.

You would like these picklists to be averaged together with a formula so that you can report out the score over time. You create a formula field that returns Text, like in Figure 5-25.

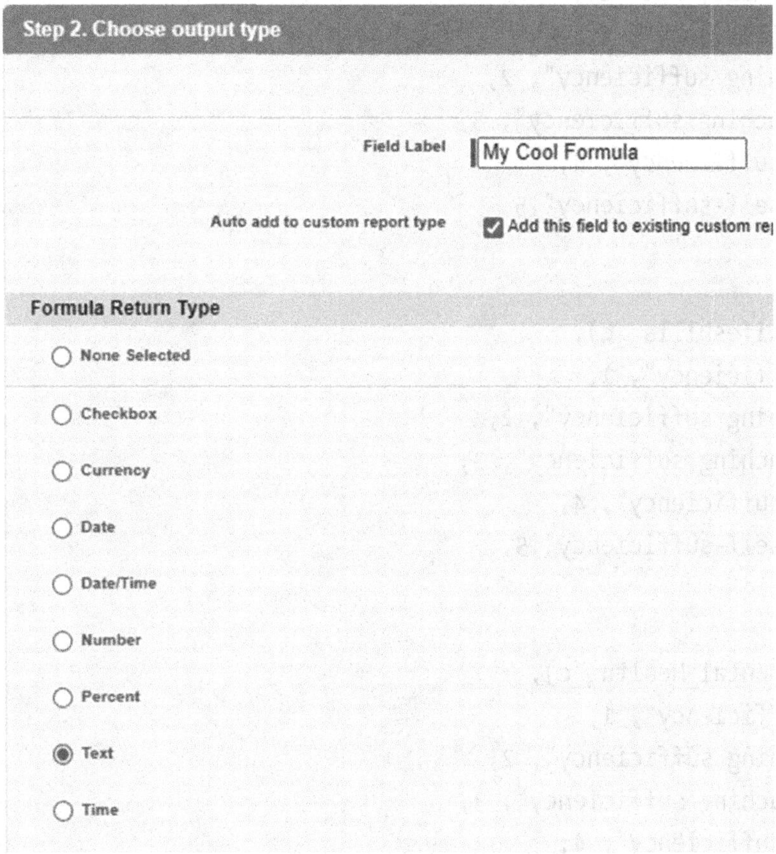

Figure 5-25. *Selecting text as the formula return type*

In the formula, you write the following:

```
CASE(TEXT(Housing__c),
"1 - No sufficiency", 1,
"2 - Beginning sufficiency", 2,
"3 - Approaching sufficiency", 3,
"4 - Near sufficiency", 4,
"5 - Full self-sufficiency",5,
0)
+
CASE(TEXT(Employment__c),
"1 - No sufficiency", 1,
"2 - Beginning sufficiency", 2,
"3 - Approaching sufficiency", 3,
"4 - Near sufficiency", 4,
"5 - Full self-sufficiency",5,
0)
+
CASE(TEXT(Lifeskills__c),
"1 - No sufficiency", 1,
"2 - Beginning sufficiency", 2,
"3 - Approaching sufficiency", 3,
"4 - Near sufficiency", 4,
"5 - Full self-sufficiency",5,
0)
+
CASE(TEXT(Mental_Health__c),
"1 - No sufficiency", 1,
"2 - Beginning sufficiency", 2,
"3 - Approaching sufficiency", 3,
"4 - Near sufficiency", 4,
"5 - Full self-sufficiency",5,
0)
+
CASE(TEXT(Safety__c),
"1 - No sufficiency", 1,
```

```
"2 - Beginning sufficiency", 2,
"3 - Approaching sufficiency", 3,
"4 - Near sufficiency", 4,
"5 - Full self-sufficiency",5,
0))
```

This formula uses a CASE Statement to look at each picklist. (CASE here is a formula function, not to be confused with the Case object in Salesforce.)

This formula takes the selected picklist value and turns it to text using the TEXT() function. Then, the next part of the function provides the text (e.g., "1 - No sufficiency"), and if the picklist matches the text, it replaces it with the number provided.

The very last number at the bottom (0 in this example) is the number used as the default if no value matches. What this means is that the CASE Statement converts each picklist into a number and then sums them all together (notice the + in between each of the CASE statements).

You can now use this formula to report the score of your assessment.

Intermediate Examples

Pulling Data from Related Objects

Formulas don't just have to look at the object you create them on. One of the most important uses is for pulling information from a related object. For example, NCCM includes a Service Delivery object. That object is used when you are delivering a service to a client, like a counseling session.

Let's say that it is important to pull the Number_of_Household_Members field from the Account that is connected to the Client on the service delivery so that you can report on the quantity of services provided and the size of the household that received them. Rather than using automation to pull this data, you can simply create a formula field and populate it like this:

pmdm__Account__r.npsp__Number_of_Household_Members__c

You'll notice the Account__r reference. This is used when you are getting a reference from a related object, while __c is used for a custom field on the same object. Note that custom means both fields you create and those that come from Salesforce packages you install, so NCCM and PMM also create fields on objects that end in __c.

Overdue for Appointment Visual Reminder

Formulas can also be used with images to create visual reminders. Let's assume you are an intimate partner violence organization that organizes group counseling sessions. Each time you have a counseling session, an automation populates the date of that counseling session and the next expected counseling session on their Contact record.

You would like a quick visual way to tell when today's date is newer than their next expected appointment. This means that the client has not been in for an appointment. This formula would look like this:

```
IF( Next_Expected_Appointment >= TODAY(), IMAGE("/img/samples/color_red.
gif","Alert", 20, 20),"")
```

This would produce a red square roughly 20x20 pixels when the next expected appointment date has passed today's date. This visual reminder can be used in reports and list views and embedded on the page layout so that it can be quickly referenced. This is shown in Figure 5-26.

Name ↑	Account Name	Phone	Email	Alert ↑
Lee Destiny...	Munoz Household	☎ +1 (211) 726-2		
Mary Harris...	Harrison Househ...	☎ +11018661179		
Max Potter	Potter Household			■
name	name Household			
New1 New1	New1 Household	☎ +38097111999		

Figure 5-26. *An alert square created with a formula, shown in a List View*

Client Age at Intake

Another common situation that is encountered is the need to determine the age of a client at intake when the program is one that they can start if they are below a certain age. For example, many foster care programs allow services for youth up to 25, as long as they were initiated before the client turned 18.

In this case, you can use the following formula:

```
(DATEVALUE((CUST_CREATED_DATE))- FK_CNTC_BIRTHDATE)/365
```

Here, CUST_CREATED_DATE is the date the intake was created, while FK_CNTC_BIRTHDATE is the client's birthday.

Advanced Examples

Nested Fields

You can nest a variety of fields inside a formula to create more complex ones. Let's say you wanted to assign complex intakes to your most experienced staff member, less complex ones to a second staff member, and the simplest cases to an intern.

You could use the following formula to evaluate Intake records to determine if they should be classified as Complex, Intermediate, or Simple.

```
IF (AND (Age < 18,
CONTAINS (CASE (Risk_Factors__c, "Suicidal Ideation", "Complex", "Homicide
Ideation", "Complex"), "Complex")),
IF(ISPICKVAL(Type, "Crisis"), "Complex",
IF(OR (ISPICKVAL (Type, "Counseling"),
ISPICKVAL(Type, "Emotional Support")), "Intermediate", "Simple")),
"Simple")
```

This formula looks complex, but it evaluates a number of elements. First, if the age of the client is less than 18 and the Risk_Factors__c field contains Suicidal Ideation or Homicide Ideation, the crisis is automatically classified as Complex.

Otherwise, if the Type field has been set as Crisis, the case is marked as Complex. If the type field is set to Counseling, the field is set to Intermediate, and if it is set to Emotional Support, it is set to Simple.

Formulas in Reports

Now that we've learned how to make basic formulas, it is important to know that you can use them in reports. There are a couple of ways to do this. The first is to simply make a regular formula field. It will be included as a column on your report.

The other way to leverage formulas in reports is to take advantage of special report formulas and features. These include Bucket Columns, Row-Level Formulas, and Summary Formulas.

Bucket Column

A bucket column allows you to "bucket" values into a single category. The simplest way to imagine a bucket column is age. If you have an age column, you may not want to report individual ages but rather see them as 0-18, 18-35, 36-49, and so on. A bucket column allows you to do this. A bucket column is shown in Figure 5-27.

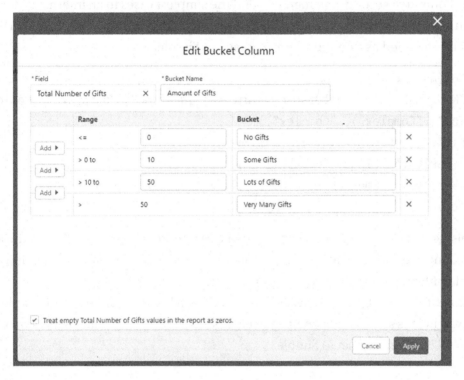

Figure 5-27. *An example of a bucket column for the total number of donations a client has made*

Row-Level Formulas

A row-level formula is very similar to a standard formula. This formula applies across each row, leveraging the columns that are available. This formula will be applied to the data on each row.

One example of a row-level formula is one that calculates the length of time a Case was open. The Age field reports this same data, but let's say you are currently tracking Case Age in hours, but for the purpose of this report, you need the number of days.

Since the Case already contains both of these fields, it is simple as CREATED_ DATEONLY - CLOSED_DATEONLY. You could create this as a standard field, but if you know you only need it on an ad hoc basis, then a row-level formula is simple and quicker than creating a dedicated field and formula for this purpose and helps keep your objects from getting cluttered with many formulas created for one-off purposes.

Summary Formulas

Summary formulas, unlike row-level formulas, apply to multiple records. The Summary Formula editor is shown in Figure 5-28.

Figure 5-28. *Editing a Summary Formula*

Summary formulas require you to have grouped your data in some way. Although the formula screen looks very familiar, the way the formula is applied is different. This becomes more clear when you actually select a field. For each field you select in the formula builder, you need to choose one of the following calculations to be performed on it:

- Sum: This is all of the values added up.

- Average: This is the mean, which is all of the values added up, divided by the number of rows.

- Min: The lowest value in the rows.

- Max: The highest value in the rows.

- Unique: The number of unique values in the list.

- Median: This is the median, which is the central value in the list.

You can use summary values to perform a variety of calculations that, without these techniques, would require you to export data to Excel.

Validation Rules

Validation rules allow you to apply the power of formulas to creating new records. With a validation rule in place, data is checked against the formula before it is saved. This means that you can ensure that the data meets certain standards for completeness or correctness before you save the record.

If the data you're inputting fails the validation rule, you can display a message either at the top of the screen or at the site of the error and give users the opportunity to fix the error before they save.

A validation rule looks very similar to the field-level formulas we've looked at, except that you create them by going to the Object and then clicking Validation Rules. After clicking New, you're prompted to give the rule a name, a description, a formula, the message to display upon the error, and where it should display.

Example Validation Rules

Validation rules, like other formulas, can be simple or complex.

Recording the Language of Non-English Calls

You might have a call center that requires you to indicate if the call was in a non-English language by checking a checkbox called Non_English_Language__c. If so, you need to select a language from the Other_Language__c picklist. That validation rule would look like this:

```
AND (Non_English_Language__c ,
ISBLANK(TEXT( Other_Language__c )))
```

Ensuring Crisis Calls Have Documentation

Or, you may have a situation where you want to make sure that when the Risk Level is set to High that the Deescalation Information field is filled out. That would look like this:

```
AND(
  ISPICKVAL( Risk_Level__c, "High" ),
  ISBLANK(Deescalation_Information__c))
```

Ensuring Closed Cases Cannot Be Edited

If you use Cases to manage the data entry procedure, you can take advantage of the fact that Salesforce provides the IsClosed checkbox to track whether the Case is closed. By creating a validation rule that is simply "IsClosed," it will prevent the Case from being edited if IsClosed is checked.

Other Considerations for Data Input

Your program evaluations are only as good as the data you put into the system. It is valuable no matter what your role that you spend some time thinking about how you want users to provide information and to put in "guardrails" in the form of formulas, validation rules, and other automation to ensure that the fewest opportunities for invalid or incorrect information are available to users.

If you make their lives easier, this preparation comes back to you in spades when users are able to complete their data entry quickly and efficiently and you can rely on that data for the impact measurement and outcome evaluation activities that you need to do.

Figure 5-29 shows a simple validation rule that prevents you from creating a Program Engagement where the Start Date is after the End Date of the client's enrollment.

Figure 5-29. *A validation rule from Program Management Module*

Certifications and Additional Learning

Salesforce has numerous opportunities for developing your skills in building reports and dashboards if you are interested in enhancing your skill in this area. On Salesforce's free Trailhead learning platform, you'll find the Salesforce Lightning Experience Reports and Dashboards Specialist superbadge.

This superbadge covers everything that we've talked about in this chapter in a practical way so you can continue to develop your fluency. This is shown in Figure 5-30.

Superbadge

Lightning Experience Reports & Dashboards Specialist
Completed March 24, 2019

Design powerful reports and dashboards to shine a light on your data.

Figure 5-30. *The Lightning Experience and Dashboards Specialist superbadge I earned*

If you decide you want a certification, Salesforce also offers the Tableau CRM and Einstein Discovery Consultant which goes beyond the built-in Salesforce reporting tools into the use of Tableau CRM and the suite of Einstein tools, some of which are covered later in this book.

Strategies for Collecting Data

There are a number of ways you can get your data into Salesforce. When you created your data model and built the objects and fields you needed, you gave your staff the tools they need to do direct data entry into Salesforce.

If you create a Survey object in Salesforce, you can distribute paper surveys to your clients and then store the results in Salesforce. These are good options for events or service deliveries where people will be in person and can quickly fill out the survey and leave it in a way that doesn't obviously link it back to themselves.

In a previous section, we looked at how you can use fields on the Assessment object in Salesforce to score assessment tools as well. By creating distinct Record Types for each assessment you want to track, you'll be able to have different assessments on the same object and have them be scored independently of each other.

Every Salesforce org also has access to an Experience Cloud. This is a web-based portal that is a front end to your Salesforce environment.

If you want people to be able to create an account in this portal, you'll need Experience Cloud licenses, but you can create an unauthenticated view that people can access for free.

In this unauthenticated Experience Cloud, participants can fill out forms or look up information. Although they can't get the information back out or look up the status of their request (because that would require an authenticated part of the portal be built out with the associated licenses), you can use this to allow web-based survey responses from clients, as shown in Figure 5-31.

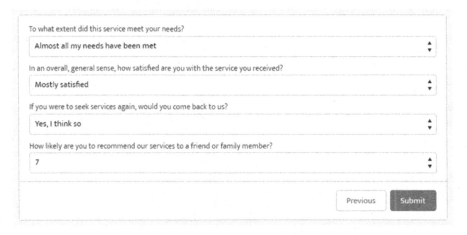

Figure 5-31. *An example of a Salesforce Experience Cloud survey in an unauthenticated view*

Once you have the data in Salesforce, you can begin analyzing it. In the next chapter, we will look at how you can take all of this data that you are bringing into the system and begin mining it for insights, understanding the impact, and evaluating the outputs and outcomes.

Conclusion

In this chapter, we looked at how to build your framework inside Salesforce. By using the tools available in Salesforce like objects, fields, validation rules, and formulas, you have built a strong data model allowing you to collect the information that you need.

In the next chapter, we will learn how to use the data we have collected to comprehensively evaluate your impact both qualitatively and quantitatively on the way to reaching your impact measurement goals.

Evaluating Impact

After building your data model, it is time to apply that data model. That is the focus of this chapter, where we will practice tying outputs to outcomes, evaluating the impact qualitatively and quantitatively using various frameworks, and then exploring how to make changes that improve impact.

Evaluating Impact Qualitatively

Qualitative methods are ways of examining information that is not numerical. This can include a wide variety of case studies, interviews, testimonials, surveys, and other data that can't be analyzed numerically or with traditional statistics.

Many people who learn and are comfortable with quantitative methods really struggle to work qualitatively. This is a "fuzzier" way of analyzing information where there's not necessarily a single right answer. Two people analyzing a qualitative dataset may come to different - but both correct - interpretations of what the data means. This kind of ambiguity can make number-focused people uncomfortable.

If you're one of these people, try to resist the urge to focus solely on quantitative data. If you do, you'll be missing a lot of nuance and value that comes from people being able to express their experiences in their own words, which can often be key to finding new insights - insights that would be lost if they were expressed as a number.

In this chapter, we will look at several methods of collecting and analyzing qualitative data to find insights. These include surveys (which can be both quantitative and qualitative), case studies, testimonials, interviews, and focus groups.

© Dustin MacDonald 2023
D. MacDonald, *Impact Measurement and Outcomes Evaluation Using Salesforce for Nonprofits*, https://doi.org/10.1007/978-1-4842-9708-7_6

Analyzing Qualitative Survey Results

Surveys, as noted earlier, can be both qualitative and quantitative. If you've ever completed a survey where you answered a question like "How likely are you to recommend this product to a friend" on a Likert scale of 1 to 5 where 5 is "Would definitely recommend" and 1 is "Would definitely *not* recommend," you have experienced a quantitative survey, shown in Figure 6-1.

Figure 6-1. *A Likert-based survey[1]*

Qualitative surveys are different. They focus on the human experience. The questions in a qualitative survey are more likely to be open ended, meaning they can't be answered with yes or no.

"Did you enjoy the movie" is an example of a closed-ended question. It asks for a specific piece of information and can be answered with yes or no. "What is your date of birth" is also a close-ended question, because it asks for a specific piece of information. You can't say yes or no, but you also can't provide any other details.

In contrast, open-ended questions ask for feelings, emotions, and experiences. They cannot be answered with a simple yes or no. Examples of open-ended questions would include the following:

---

[1] https://pixabay.com/photos/opinion-poll-opinion-polling-survey-1594962

- What was your experience with the intake process like?

- How can we improve the client experience?

- Which services do you like? Which did you dislike?

- What other feedback can we integrate into the program?

These questions are open and promote individuals to share more than they would with close-ended questions.

When designing an open-ended survey, it is important to ask yourself a few questions. First, what information are you trying to collect? This is critical before you begin designing the survey because knowing where you are going to end up helps you ask the right kinds of questions.

Surveys can be used for a variety of purposes. These include designing a new program, where you might want to know what sort of services or benefits people would like to get out of the program or updating existing programs. In the latter, you want to know how things people have already experienced can be changed. If you're completing a logic model or theory of change, a survey can help you understand what changes individuals experienced throughout the process.

Although you can probably find surveys online that are like the kind of information you want to collect, this is one of the few situations that it usually makes sense to design your own. By carefully targeting the survey questions, you can ensure that you are collecting exactly the kind of information you want while not bothering people with information that is irrelevant and doesn't help you advance your goals.

Once you know what kind of survey you are completing, you need to make sure that it is targeted appropriately to your audience. This involves several components: time commitment, reading level, technology, and appropriateness of questions.

Time Commitment

Time commitment: Have you ever agreed to complete a survey only to find out that it will take 30 minutes that you don't have right now? You likely closed the survey and went on your way. The person who created the survey may have appreciated your insights, but it was just too much time.

It's important to calibrate the length of the survey to the people who will be completing it. A white-collar technology professional sitting in their office may have more time to complete a survey than a harried single mother or an unhoused individual who needs to focus on their immediate survival needs.

Reading Level

The reading level of the people who will be completing your surveys is important. If the reading level is too high, individuals may be frustrated or confused by the questions and either not provide the answers you are looking for or simply not continue with the survey at all.

There are several ways to estimate reading level. One of the simplest is to have several potential survey recipients read the survey and tell you if they think the reading level is appropriate. This has the advantage of targeting the exact population you are hoping to complete the survey, though you run the risk of your sample telling you the reading level was fine to avoid admitting that they are struggling with the material.

Another option to estimate reading levels is called the Flesch Reading Ease. There are lots of websites online that will do this calculation for you.

The full calculation is as follows:

206.835 - 1.015 × (number of words ÷ number of sentences) - 84.6 × (number of syllables ÷ number of words).

It's calculated with the following steps:

1. Select a sample and count the sentences in it (e.g., 100 words).

2. Divide the number of words by the number of sentences.

3. Multiply the output from step 2 by 1.015 and set this number aside.

4. Count the number of syllables in the 100 words, and divide it by 100.

5. Multiply the output from step 4 by 84.6 and set this number aside.

6. Add the output from step 3 and step 5 together.

7. Subtract the output from step 6 from 206.835.

The final number is the Flesch Reading Ease score, which ranges from 0 to 100 where a higher number is better. Most newspapers are written at a fifth grade reading level (a 90 or higher Flesch score.)

You can see from Table 6-1 how the Flesch Reading Ease score translates to reading ease.

Table 6-1. *The Flesch Reading Ease score*

Reading ease	Grade	Difficulty
90–100	5	Very easy
80–89	6	Easy
70–79	7	Fairly easy
60–69	8–9	Standard
50–59	10–12	Fairly difficult
30–49	College student	Difficult
0–29	College graduate	Very difficult

Example Reading Ease

To demonstrate the calculation of reading ease, I've taken a passage from earlier in this chapter. Here are 100 words:

Reading level: The reading level of the people who will be completing your surveys is important. If the reading level is too high, individuals may be frustrated or confused by the questions and either not provide the answers you are looking for or simply not continue with the survey at all.

There are several ways to estimate reading level. One of the simplest is to have several potential survey recipients read the survey and tell you if they think the reading level is appropriate. This has the advantage of targeting the exact population you are hoping to complete the survey.

Now we'll go through the same seven steps earlier:

1. Select a sample and count the sentences in it: five sentences.

2. Divide the number of words by the number of sentences: 100 words / 5 sentences = 20.

3. Multiply the output from step 2 by 1.015 and set this number aside: 20 x 1.015 = 20.3.

4. Count the number of syllables in the 100 words, and divide it by 100: 159 / 100 = 1.59.

5. Multiply the output from step 4 by 84.6 and set this number aside: 1.59 x 84.6 = 134.514.

6. Add the output from step 3 and step 5 together = 154.814.

7. Subtract the output from step 6 from 206.835: 206.835 – 154.814 = 52.02.

A 52 is considered difficult to read, or a 10th to 12th grade reading level.

Technology

There are a variety of options for sending and receiving surveys. A Salesforce Experience Cloud can be configured to allow individuals to complete surveys that become records in Salesforce (more on that in Chapter 7).

Salesforce also provides a survey tool through Salesforce Feedback Management. This is a full-cycle feedback and survey management system that competes with professional survey tools like Qualtrics and SurveyMonkey. The downside is that you get only 300 survey responses in the lifetime of the organization, before you need to get licenses and begin paying.

The survey builder is shown in Figure 6-2.

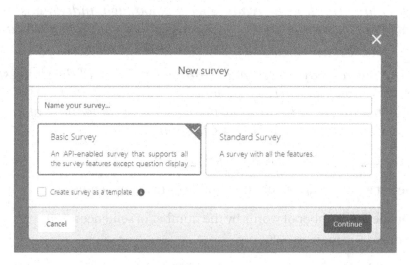

Figure 6-2. *The Salesforce Feedback Management survey builder*

Paper surveys are, of course, also options which can then be added into Salesforce by hand. It is important that you calibrate your surveys to ensure they reflect the population you are working with.

If your population does not use computers, a computerized survey is unlikely to have a good response rate. On the other hand, if your population is young and tech savvy, they may strongly prefer a computerized survey to one that they have to fill out on paper and then give to someone to enter the system.

Appropriateness of Questions

In the same way that the technology used should be targeted at your client population, the questions should also be appropriate. In addition to matching the reading level of your participants, you also want to make sure that you are asking questions that the clients can answer at the time you are giving them the survey.

For example, it might be inappropriate to ask an individual what their experience with a program is after the first session, when they expect to be in the program for several months. Instead, waiting until they've had enough time to experience the program will ensure a more accurate response.

One way that you can assess the appropriateness of questions is to ask some trusted clients to look at the questions before you begin administering the survey more widely. They will be able to advise you about whether the questions are appropriate and point out any situations where you may have a blind spot that could offend or upset an individual receiving the survey.

In general, leveraging the benefit of clients with lived experience who are interested in helping the organization is a valuable way for them to give back and to assist in the development of surveys, assessments, case studies, and other materials that can help.

Collecting Case Studies and Testimonials

Case studies and testimonials are a great way for you to learn directly from your clients and other stakeholders. While testimonials are usually collected specifically to highlight something positive, case studies are more demonstrative and may include positive and negative experiences.

A case study is a useful way for you to demonstrate something to individuals who might be interested in using your product or service. This can be in the form of a "white paper" where you do a write-up of a client's experience or a specific situation (e.g., how you handled an emergency housing situation), a video where a client or former client walks you through their experience, or a presentation that you might deliver to community groups.

The important things to keep in mind when preparing a case study are that you use a generic example, that you have consent to tell the story, and that you connect the case study to the next steps with a call to action. These elements will be reviewed more in the following.

Use a Generic Example

It's important when you write a case study that you pick an example that is generic enough to apply to a broad cross section of people. As a housing organization, for example, you may have situations where you have handled unique situations and have resolved them using creative problem solving and highly trained employees. These are great for marketing purposes, but they don't help individuals trying to understand what your organization does on a day-to-day basis.

A case study based on how your staff helped a client whose house burned down get housing in 24 hours is a much better example for a case study than a situation where you helped a celebrity who found themselves without accommodation. The second may have seemed interesting but doesn't represent a good opportunity to tell people about the organization.

Consent

The importance of consent cannot be overstated when using any kind of testimonial or case study in public-facing materials. If you don't have the permission of the individual whose story you are telling, not only can it represent a public relations issue or even legal exposure to the organization, but it can also severely retraumatize the individual.

I know of an individual who regularly used services of mental health organizations in the area. They had complaints about the service quality and spoke to the newspaper about doing a story. While they had consented to their name and story being used, they didn't expect that a large photo of themselves with many self-injury scars would appear alongside the story that was distributed in the newspaper's large catchment area.

Figure 6-3, a picture of my cat as a Salesforce contact, is a good reminder of the importance of consent.

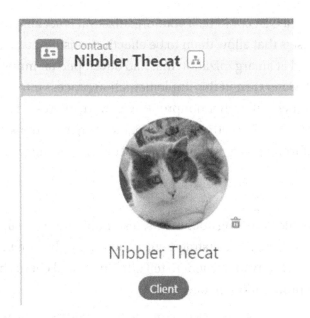

Figure 6-3. *Owning a cat is an excellent lesson in consent*

Be very careful when you collect client consents to ensure that they understand exactly what they are providing their consent for, including how their information will be used or could be used in the future, and that they understand how they can revoke consent if they decide that it doesn't work for them.

Call to Action

A Call to Action (CTA) is a request that an individual do something. In any sales situation, you need a call to action to tell the consumer of the information what to do next. A case study is, in its own way, a sales document because you're demonstrating your organization's expertise and ability to handle situations to some end. That end can depend on the specific reason you prepared the case study.

Some case studies may be prepared by organizations who are seeking funding, in which case the CTA may include contacting the organization's development or fundraising staff to find out how to donate.

If your case study's purpose is to encourage clients to sign up for the program, your CTA should include information on how to get involved, who to talk to to initiate the outreach or whatever that next step looks like.

A final example of a CTA could be if your organization is seeking to consult. Many nonprofits have skillsets that allow them to be effective consultants to other nonprofits. For example, I worked at an organization that had developed an innovative crisis chat and text program. We later turned this implementation process into the focus of a case study and consulted with other nonprofits who were interested in duplicating the program. In this case, the CTA on that white paper told organizations how to get in touch with us and what information we would need to begin consulting for them.

Testimonials

Unlike case studies which are long documents, testimonials are usually small and short, as shown in Figure 6-4. Less than a paragraph, sometimes only a single sentence, a testimonial is an opportunity for a client to tell other potential clients how much they appreciate your nonprofit's mission or services.

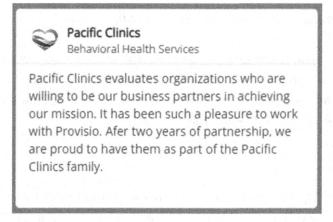

Figure 6-4. *An example of a testimonial*

Testimonials make useful additions to your website, your marketing material, your annual report, and other public-facing materials. Before I joined the board of a literacy organization, seeing the testimonials on the nonprofit's website was critical: individuals telling stories of how they couldn't get their driver's license because they couldn't read the manual or they couldn't tell their kids bedtime stories until they got involved with the organization and how it changed their life were very compelling.

Like case studies, you will want to ensure you have consent to use the individual's name (and photo if applicable) and for how long.

Facilitating Interviews and Focus Groups

Interviews and focus groups are related but distinct ways of collecting information from small groups. These are great tools to use to get detailed feedback from your constituents. This can be used at the beginning of a program to determine what your constituents want or after they've been through the program to get feedback to change things for the future.

Interviews

Interviews are conducted one-on-one. There are semi-structured and structured interviews. A structured interview is one where you have a fixed set of questions and you only ask and collect the answers related to those questions. A semi-structured interview is one where the interview starts with the fixed questions but can allow the conversation to veer off into questions or topics that are not included.

A structured interview is a good choice if you are interviewing clients about a program that will be launched. This ensures that you collect the minimum necessary information to guide the process. When interviewing clients after they've gone through the program, a semi-structured interview is a better choice to ensure you're not limiting your client's responses based on the fixed questions you came up with.

Before conducting interviews, it's important that you ask potential participants for their permission to answer questions. You should ensure that they understand how long the process will take and that they can revoke their consent or stop participating at any time. They should also understand the goal of the interview to help them be most comfortable.

Focus Groups

Interviews are usually one-on-one events. A focus group is a group interview process. Unlike other kinds of interviews where the focus is on the specific questions asked and the responses received, focus groups benefit from the group dynamic and the interactions between the different participants.

Focus groups are commonly used to test groups of reactions to things like new marketing campaigns, test screening of movies, or exploring whether a new program or service would meet the needs of the people receiving it.

The size of an effective focus group is between six and ten people. A group that is too small will not have enough variability to stimulate good conversation, while a group that is too big may not allow enough discussion to happen between different participants.

The participants should be like the people whose opinions you are interested in. For example, if you are focus grouping a crisis counseling program for homeless individuals, having the participants be wealthy individuals who have never experienced homelessness would not be effective. Instead, having individuals who have been unhoused within the last 12 months (to include those who are in transitional housing now or are actively unhoused) would be much more representative of the experience.

The role of the moderator, who is the facilitator of the discussion, is to ensure a comfortable and safe environment. Participants should be informed of how the focus group will function, including housekeeping information like the duration.

During the discussion, the moderator asks questions to start the discussion and tries to keep it on track by returning to the topic at hand. Recording the session with a Dictaphone or similar device is probably the easiest way to ensure that all information is recorded.

After the session, you can review the recording and turn it into the notes and insights that you will take into any modifications that you make to the program.

Focus groups are generally underused in nonprofits when compared with for-profit businesses. Part of this may be the difficulty of gathering consent and a desire not to exploit your clients; however, there are few ways that are better to quickly get a group read on something than a focus group.

Evaluating Impact Quantitatively

Evaluating impact quantitatively involves using numerical tools to get a more empirical or mathematical understanding of the impact that you've achieved. This involves a variety of tools including assessments, statistical analysis, and similar techniques.

Entry and Exit Assessments

One of the simplest ways to evaluate your impact quantitatively is by asking people to complete an entry and an exit assessment. This can be as simple as a single question you ask at the beginning and the end of a service or as complex as a validated assessment tool that collects standardized information.

Many nonprofits ask individuals to complete an assessment tool as part of the intake process. Very few ask individuals to complete the same assessment as part of the exit process. This robs you of valuable opportunities to collect this data.

Figure 6-5 shows a stack of papers, a common sight in organizations that use paper-based assessments.

Figure 6-5. *Representing a stack of assessments in a case management agency*[2]

If you don't currently collect any intake data, you should look at a tool like the Arizona Self-Sufficiency Matrix (ASSM), the Beck Depression Inventory Version 2 (BDI-II), or similar to give you a starting point. These tools take only a couple minutes to administer and can be repeated over time to give you the data you need.

You can also administer assessment tools to employees. As a trainer at a crisis liner who facilitated our basic crisis line training, we required each trainee to complete a pretest to collect information on their knowledge of suicide prevention techniques, their attitudes toward suicide and suicidal behavior, and their confidence in their ability to handle different crisis situations. When we repeated the same survey at the end of each training session, we saw a marked improvement as people developed the skills, knowledge, and attitudes necessary to effectively intervene with individuals in crisis.

---

[2] https://pixabay.com/photos/files-files-shelf-paper-office-4440841/

Analyzing Quantitative Survey Results

Once you have your survey data, you need to analyze it. This can be done in Excel, R, Python, or a variety of other tools. If you don't have anyone available to help who has statistics experience or education, don't fret. Although it can be very helpful to proof your outcomes if you have a statistics background, it's not necessary.

Returning to the crisis line example from earlier, we administered a simple "How upset are you?" question to individuals when their chat connected. We didn't use this data to sort or triage (and we made that clear to participants) but for our own data analysis.

After the interaction was over, which lasted an average of 45 minutes, we asked participants again how they were feeling. The average person who reached out for support was feeling 3.4 out of 5, where a higher number means more distress. After 45 minutes of talking to one of our trained crisis responders, they were only at a 2.5 level of distress.

The percentage difference between 3.4 and 2.5 can be determined with a simple formula: new – old / old. In this case

$$2.5 - 3.4 / 3.4$$

$$= -0.9 / 3.4$$

$$= -0.26$$

Or a 26% reduction in distress. That's a significant reduction for a single conversation of 45 minutes.

To use a different example, you might have people complete the Arizona Self Sufficiency Matrix (ASSM) which involves 15 domains, marked from 1 to 5 where 5 is completely self-sufficient in that domain and 1 is no self-sufficiency at all. Higher scores are better, and the maximum score you can achieve is 75.

You might ask each client or their case manager to complete the ASSM on a weekly basis as they proceed through counseling. A client's ASSM might be 24 on week 0 (their very first meeting with the case manager), 35 after 3 months, and 49 when they decide to exit the program. If you decide to go with fewer domains (maybe your program only looks at 3 or 5 or 10 of the 15 domains), then your maximum score will be lower.

In this example, we are using all 15 domains. A score of 24 across 15 domains means that the average score for those domains is as follows:

$$24 / 15 \text{ domains} = 1.6$$

A score of 1.6 out of 5 means this client lacks significant self-sufficiency. It's clear that in most areas of their life, there is major improvement to be made. Looking at our 3-month mark, when they've had perhaps 12 weekly sessions or more, our self-sufficiency score has risen to 75.

$$35 / 15 \text{ domains} = 2.3$$

Now, 2.3 out of 5 may not seem like much but that is a huge improvement. Returning to our previous percentage change formula, we can see that 2.3 – 1.6 / 1.6 = 0.44 or an increase of 44% in their self-sufficiency.

When they decide to exit the program, they've got a total self-sufficiency score of 49, which represents an average score in each domain of 3.3 out of 5. Not bad! And from their original score of 24, they improved by 104%, more than double!

This is a really easy way to put improvements in client functioning and other impact measures into a way that anyone can understand. Additionally, it requires tools no more complex than a calculator or a pad of paper to accomplish.

Statistical Measurement Techniques

If you decide to use statistics to prove the outcomes that you achieved, you'll be moving into more advanced mathematics and reasoning. This is a great step for an organization that is ready to move to the next level in their impact and outcome measurement by showing that the outcomes they are achieved are not just the result of random chance but truly the program or service that you created.

In the future, you might even choose to publish the work that you've done by submitting it to a scientific journal where it can undergo peer review and become part of the literature, so that others can benefit from the model you've validated.

We'll use a simple example of what is called a dependent sample t-test to show how to use statistics to demonstrate the value of your program. If we were examining individuals who had or had not received an intervention (such as a control group and an experimental group), we would use a two-sample t-test.

Returning to our previous example, individuals who had no interaction with our program had an average distress level of 3.4. We know that individuals who spoke to a crisis worker had an average distress level of 2.5. We want to know whether this change is the result of chance or the result of the intervention (the crisis support that we provided.)

To complete a dependent sample t-test, there are five steps:

- Define your null hypothesis and alternative hypothesis.

- Decide on an alpha value. This is the level of risk that you are willing to accept that the change occurred by chance. A common alpha value is 0.05. This means that there is a 5% chance that the change was caused by chance. You can go further to 0.01 (1% chance) if you wish, though you don't often see values outside of these two numbers.

- Check for independence.

- Check for normality and other assumptions.

- Run the test and examine the results.

We are now going to look at each of these.

Define Your Null Hypothesis and Alternative Hypothesis

When doing a statistical analysis, you need to define two hypotheses or assumptions about what is happening. The null hypothesis is that nothing is happening or that there is no connection between the items you are studying.

For example, if you are doing a study looking at grades and number of hours studied, your null hypothesis would be "There is no relationship between hours studied and the grade on the final exam."

The other hypothesis is the alternative hypothesis. This is the hypothesis that the two items you are looking at are related.

In our grades example, the alternative hypothesis is that "There is a relationship between hours studied and the grade on the final exam." At this point, we may not be certain how hours studying affect the grade on the final exam. In that case, we will conduct a two-tailed t-test so we can find out if hours studying cause the grade to increase or decrease.

If we are certain that we know it will only move in one direction, we can do a one-tailed t-test. This gives us more statistical power (making it more likely we will detect a statistically significant difference if one exists), at the expense of only being able to check in one direction.

Returning to our crisis example, our hypotheses are as follows:

- H_0 (null hypothesis): Distress level of people after talking to a crisis counselor is equal to the distress level of people before visiting.

- H_a (alternative hypothesis): Distress level of people after talking to a crisis counselor is less than the distress level of people before visiting.

Decide on an Alpha Value

Now we need to decide on an alpha value. The alpha value or α is the significance level. With the most common value of 0.05, we would expect to obtain a statistically significant result when it was the null hypothesis 5% of the time.

An alpha value of 0.05 achieves a good balance between reliability and the sample size needed, because a lower significance value requires more data to ensure confidence in the results. We will use the alpha of 0.05 for our example.

Check for Independence

Next, we need to check for independence. In some situations, you can run a specific test of independence like the Chi-square test of independence. For dependent t-tests, this is not the case. Instead, we need to understand how the data was collected. We want to use what is called in a random sample without replacement.

This means that you choose a random selection of crisis calls and that once you've chosen one, it cannot be selected again. (This is the no replacement part.) If you had allowed replacement, that would mean that you could potentially choose the same crisis call multiple times, thus affecting the validity of the results.

Check for Normality and Other Assumptions

Next, we need to check for a variety of assumptions. These assumptions include the following:

- The dependent variable is continuous.

- The observations are independent of each other (we already checked for this earlier so we don't need to repeat it here).

- The dependent variable should be normally distributed.

- The dependent variable should not include outliers.

CHAPTER 6　EVALUATING IMPACT

The dependent variable is the variable that is affected by what you're doing. In the "hours studied and grade on the exam" example, the dependent variable is the grade on the exam because it is influenced by the hours studied.

In the crisis call and level of distress example, the dependent variable is the level of distress. One of our assumptions is that it must be a continuous variable, which to keep things simple is a value that can have a decimal point like 1.0, 2.4, or 3.14159. The opposite would be a discrete variable which can only take on certain values like "Low," "Medium," or "High," or 1, 2, or 3.

We also want to exclude any outliers. In this particular example, they were not able to put any values below 1 or above 5, so the issue of outliers isn't present. In our hours studied example, however, if most people studied under 10 hours and one person reported studying 50 hours, that value needs to be examined to find out if it is a data entry error or otherwise does not belong.

Run the Test and Examine the Results

Finally, it is time to run the t-test and examine the results. We'll use Excel for this. I've generated some fake distress data in Table 6-2, using the RANDBETWEEN() function. To get the average difference between the pre and post values, I used the MEAN() function and STDEV.S for the standard deviation.

Table 6-2. *Some sample data for analysis*

Pre	Post	Difference
3	2	1
1	1	0
2	1	1
2	1	1
5	4	1
3	2	1
3	2	1
4	1	3
3	1	2
3	1	2
2	1	1
3	2	1
3	3	0
4	3	1
5	2	3
3	3	0
4	5	-1
5	2	3
5	3	2
1	1	0
Mean		1.15
Standard Deviation		1.09

That looks like this. Now we can use an Excel function to do our statistical test:

=T.TEST(B3:B22, C3:C22, 2, 1)

B3:B22 is the pre column, while C3 to C22 is the post column. The "2" is a reference to a two-tailed test, which allows us to see whether the value is going up or down. If you were completing a one-tailed test, you would change that to a "1".

Finally, the "1" is a reference to the type of t-test to perform. You can refer to Table 6-3.

Table 6-3. *The value used to tell Microsoft Excel which type of t-test to perform*

Value	Type
1	Paired
2	Two-sample equal variance
3	Two-sample unequal variance

Because we are performing a paired t-test, we use 1 for the type.

The output from the test is 0.00015.

This value is less than our significance value of 0.05; therefore, we can reject the null hypothesis. There is a statistically significant difference between the pre and post values meaning that our program is confirmed to be responsible for the difference that we saw.

Making Changes to Improve Impact

Improving Survey Results

Once you've received feedback from your surveys, you have some information you can use to improve your programs. Surveys are interesting because often people don't fill them out unless they're upset. This can cause a "bimodal" effect on your survey results where many of them are either a 1 out of 5 or a 5 out of 5.

Although you should read every narrative comment, you may find the most valuable information in the 2, 3, or 4 out of 5 submissions because these represent the ones where people have nuanced feedback. They acknowledge that the program has value but also can point out where the shortcomings are.

Consider administering "alumni" surveys to former clients as well. This can give you insight into people who have felt the impact of your programming on a longer scale.

Improving Assessment Results

Assessment results can be harder than surveys to improve. While surveys represent the opinions and beliefs of individuals who have been through your programs, assessments are more objective. If you are administering the VI-SPDAT or the Self Sufficiency Matrix and your client's functioning hasn't improved, that will be visible in the assessments.

One way to begin improving assessment results is to put them into a report and examine which values are the lowest to see if you can strategically target those items. For example, if many of your clients in an eating disorder program are struggling with housing, you may be able to partner with a housing organization to assist individuals in seeking out safe, reliable housing options.

Because many nonprofit grantors or funders prefer to work with organizations that have partnerships, this can also strengthen the financial position of both groups as you seek out combined funding to tackle multiple issues in your community.

Social Return on Investment

Social return on investment or SROI is another excellent way to demonstrate the impact of your program. Discussed more in Chapter 2, SROI allows you to take a theory of change and apply a dollar value to it.

This SROI ratio allows you to clearly demonstrate how money invested in your program leads to the creation of social value and savings to other stakeholders and community agencies.

A brief review of the SROI steps is included here. For a full review of the SROI process, see Chapter 2. The six steps for the SROI process are as follows:

1. Establishing the scope and identifying stakeholders

2. Mapping outputs

3. Demonstrating outcomes and giving them a value

4. Establishing impact

5. Calculating the SROI

6. Reporting, using, and embedding

The SROI process can be a one-off, but ideally should not be. Once you've completed your SROI analysis, you have a lot of data to work with. Your outputs map to your outcomes which you combine with your financial proxies, subtracting the cost of the inputs to arrive at your ratio.

By examining the inputs with the highest cost, you can begin to look for opportunities to reduce them. This is the equivalent of a business owner that looks to cut costs to improve the "bottom line" net income by cutting costs. For example, if your organization is currently led by staff, you could examine whether adding volunteers can help. In many areas, volunteers are as effective as paid staff in performing duties like helpline support, administrative work, or providing peer support.

You can also look at the outcomes that have the highest social value and try to have more of them. This is equivalent to raising the "top line" revenue of an organization. When you understand which of your activities produces the biggest social value, you can increase your focus on that program.

For example, perhaps a legal aid organization completes an SROI analysis and determines that assisting detained individuals produces the greatest amount of value. They may begin an advertising campaign to improve awareness of this program by distributing flyers to local community agencies, giving business cards to activists, and ensuring local jails and detention facilities have the organization listed in their contacts.

It is wise to repeat your SROI analysis at least as often as your strategic plan so that you can ensure you are using the most recent data on the impact you are having in the community.

Reporting on Impact

Reporting on impact is one of the most important parts of the entire data process. If you don't use the information that you collect, or don't use and disseminate it properly, you may as well have not gone through the process to collect and analyze it in the first place.

In previous sections, we learned how to evaluate the data that we collected and tweak it so that it provides maximum value. This section will focus on how to disseminate your completed analyses.

Annual Reports

Annual reports as a term can refer to two different things. First, many funders, government agencies like the IRS, and state organizations like the Secretary of State require nonprofit organizations to file annual reports. These are often in a prescribed format like Form 990 (shown in Figure 6-6), Return of Organization Exempt from Income Tax, leaving little room for creativity.

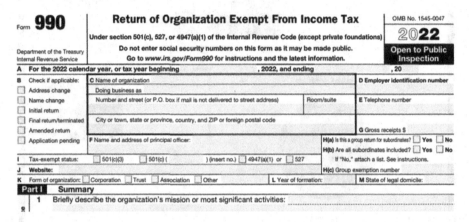

Figure 6-6. *The start of the Form 990*

Outside of these required forms, many organizations also issue a document they call an Annual Report that describes the work the organization has done in the last year. This document gives you the opportunity to report out on your impact. Figure 6-7 is an excerpt from an Annual Report.

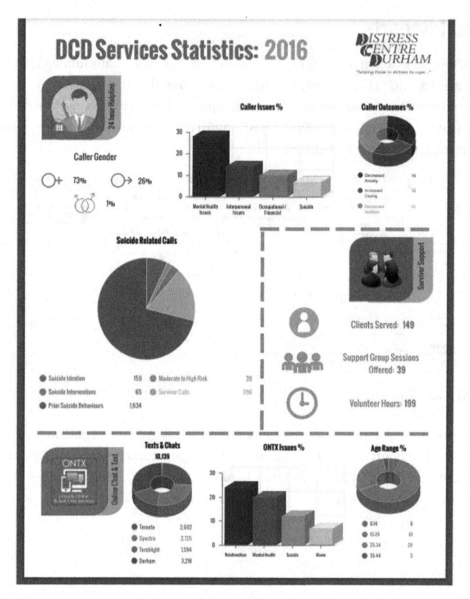

Figure 6-7. *A chart from an Annual Report*

By including both outputs (number of individuals housed, number of services provided, hours of counseling delivered, etc.) and outcomes (reduction in 9/11, increased access to hospital beds, decrease in the county suicide rate), you can show individuals and partner organizations the benefits of partnering with your organization.

If your annual report could use some improvement, find out if you have staff with a flair for graphic design. If not, I have seen several organizations having success by asking local college graphic design students to assist in creating a new Annual Report. A nominal sum (e.g., $200) along with recognition in the Annual Report can be a great combination that gives them a resume line item, while you receive the benefit of a newly designed report for a lot less money than a professional would cost.

Social Media

Social media is an increasingly important aspect of both communication and fundraising. By connecting directly with potential donors, stakeholders, and service recipients, you allow them to build the connection they may need before they begin reaching out for services. For many potential clients, fear of the unknown or worries about being judged can be enough to keep them from reaching out leaving clients underserved.

Social media can help clients feel more comfortable and even act as a funnel that can take in requests from people seeking support and route them to the right intake individuals.

Reporting on impact with social media involves regular updates on the kinds of support your organization is providing. One crisis line I was involved in would make regular updates letting people know they saved a life each day that they completed an "active rescue" for someone who had taken steps to end their life like taking pills and had received an ambulance. This helped remind individuals and funders that their work was valuable and lead to earned media as curious journalists reached out to find out more.

Social media is constantly evolving and changing. What works on LinkedIn doesn't work on Facebook or Instagram. And what worked on Instagram 2 years ago may not work today. For this reason, if your organization is big enough, you should try to acquire dedicated resources in this area.

If you can't afford a full-time social media marketer, try to carve 10 hours a week out of a staff member's role (a staff member who is interested in becoming a social media marketer!) and assist them in completing the training from HubSpot or other social media marketing platforms. This will ensure they are using industry best practices to promote the whole organization on social media in addition to specifically promoting the impact that your organization accomplishes.

Earned Media

Earned media is a term that describes newspapers, mentions on TV, writeups in other people's blogs, and any other situation where you aren't driving the interaction but instead have "earned" the mention by virtue of your organization's good work. The opposite of earned media would be something like a press release you've sent out or a guest post in a blog where you are driving the interaction.

Salesforce Standard Reporting

In the previous chapter, we did a deep dive on Salesforce reporting functionality. This reporting functionality comes out of the box, and all organizations have access to it. Unless it's been turned off deliberately, virtually all users have access to it as well.

Both PMM and NCCM come out of the box with a lot of great reports. These reports allow you to quickly pull information of interest like the number of contacts and accounts you've created, the number and quantity (e.g., hours or units) of service deliveries delivered, the attendance at Service Sessions that you've hosted, and more.

Figure 6-8 shows a Salesforce Report.

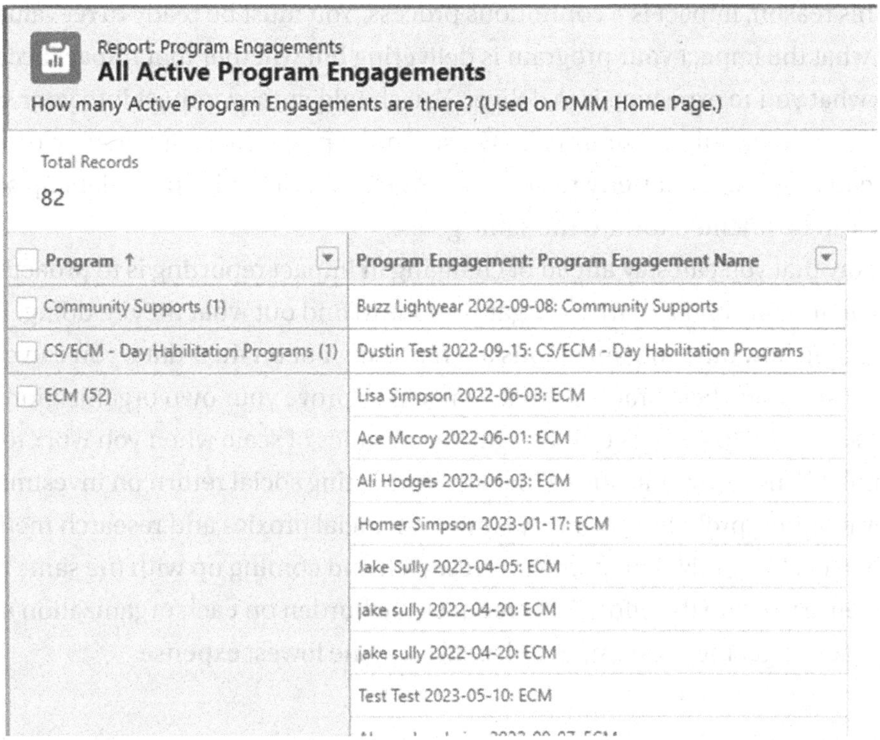

Figure 6-8. *A Salesforce Report*

These reports are excellent ways to get an understanding of the "universe" of reporting so that you can begin to understand what the system can do. From there, you can begin to build your own reports that expand on this data. If you're looking for more information on this topic and haven't read it yet, see the previous chapter for more information on reports and dashboards.

Other Issues in Evaluating Impact

Evaluating impact is not a one and done thing. You might decide that the metrics that make sense in year 1 of your program don't make sense in year 2 and beyond. Your funders may ask you for different kinds of information, necessitating a change in the kind of outcomes that you measure, and your constituents or service recipients may say that they want the program to do different things. When the program changes, the impact will also change.

For this reason, impact is a continuous process. You must be ready to reevaluate not only what the impact your program is delivering but whether that impact accurately matches what you're expecting it to deliver. You should embed impact into your strategic plan and make examining your impact measurement program a regular activity. I recommend building a quarterly review process into the activities of leadership so that everyone can be oriented toward the same goals.

One way that you can stay ahead of changing in impact reporting is to proactively reach out to funders and to partner organizations to find out what they're doing. By understanding how other organizations are reporting out on their data, you can get inspiration and trade best practices that can help improve your own organization's work.

Another reason to share is that you gain economies of scale when you work together. For example, housing organizations that are conducting social return on investment (SROI) evaluations probably have very similar financial proxies and research methods. Rather than each organization doing this research and coming up with the same proxies, it makes sense to share the effort. This reduces the burden on each organization and ensures that you get the most impactful analysis at the lowest expense.

Conclusion

Congratulations on making it through another chapter. In the previous pages, you have learned how to evaluate impact qualitatively and quantitatively, using statistical techniques and leveraging the full power of impact measurement evaluation, as well as how to adjust your processes to maximize impact.

In the next chapter, we will dive deep into the change management process to ensure your changes are accepted and implemented throughout the organization.

CHAPTER 7

The Change Management Process

In the previous chapters, we've looked at Salesforce and Nonprofit Cloud Case Management. We've also examined the basics of impact measurement and outcome evaluation as well as how to create a logic model or theory of change to document the effectiveness of the program or services that you are providing to individuals. Then, we looked at how to report and evaluate that impact so that we can make changes to improve the impact that we have and best position our organization and our clients for success.

Now, we turn our attention to change management. Change management is the process and framework used to make changes in a controlled way so that you achieve buy-in and the desired changes.

In many organizations, changes come from the top without a lot of thought about how they will be received at the bottom. This causes a lot of easily avoidable friction. In fact, one literature review looking at change management efforts estimated that as many as 70% of organizational change initiatives fail[1].

It's likely that by proceeding through this book, you will come to find yourself interested in making several changes or implementing new models, frameworks, or procedures. Before doing so, it is critical that you understand the basics of change management to ensure that these changes are accepted.

Entire books have been written on change management, and it is a fertile area of research in fields as wide as organizational behavior, public administration, leadership,

---

[1] Errida A, Lotfi B. The determinants of organizational change management success: Literature review and case study. International Journal of Engineering Business Management. 2021;13. doi:10.1177/18479790211016273

© Dustin MacDonald 2023
D. MacDonald, *Impact Measurement and Outcomes Evaluation Using Salesforce for Nonprofits*,
https://doi.org/10.1007/978-1-4842-9708-7_7

and psychology. This chapter will review some basic frameworks and tips that you can use to ensure your efforts at change in your organization do not fail.

Although there are a variety of change management models, the one featured here is the model by Anthony Mento and his colleagues. This 12-step model is comprehensive but simple enough for anyone to implement it:

1. Determine the idea and its context.

2. Define the change initiative.

3. Evaluate the climate for change.

4. Develop a change plan.

5. Identify a sponsor.

6. Prepare the recipients of change.

7. Create the cultural fit.

8. Develop and choose a change leader team.

9. Create small wins for motivation.

10. Constantly and strategically communicate the change.

11. Measure progress of the change effort.

12. Integrate lessons learned.

Next, we will look at each of these steps in detail so that you can be prepared to make changes in your own organization.

Step 1: Determine the Idea and Its Context

The very first step to change management is that there must be a change to manage! Before you begin working on the rest of the process, you must identify that a change is going to take place so that you can prepare for it. This can be harder than it seems at first glance.

Some changes are very big and obvious, such as the desire to switch to a new technology platform like Salesforce, but others are much smaller or more subtle. Does adding new fields onto a page require a change management process? It may, especially if the staff who work with that page are very resistant to changes.

Some changes occur organically or suddenly, and so you may not have the opportunity to prepare for them. For example, if a key leader leaves the organization, that may throw things into upheaval with very little notice. Or, as the organization grows, you may find yourself having to scroll down longer lists of contacts than you are used to, causing people to complain that they can't find the records they're looking for.

Other changes are more intentional. If you decide to create a new program or adjust a program because of your impact measurement or outcome evaluation activities, you will likely have more time to prepare for that change. As a staff member announces retirement in a few months, you may begin to explore how their loss will affect the organization. And as you implement planned upgrades to your Salesforce organization or other technology, you can explore how those changes will affect things.

The context that a change is occurring can also influence its adoption. If the change is made by someone new to the organization who has not established their "bona fides" or built the trust of those who are being asked to change their behavior, it is far less likely to be adopted than if it is driven by someone who is already respected. This is explored more in step 5 where you identify a sponsor.

Another element of the context of a change is the "why" behind the change. Some changes are imposed on us from external pressures like a change in funder, an update that renders software or hardware obsolete, or feedback from clients. These changes may be necessary and important, but they are based on preventing something bad from happening: rejection of a grant, an inability to use software or hardware, or poor reviews from community members.

Other changes are to help something good happen. These changes, like adopting Salesforce, simplifying processes, or adding new programs, can make staff lives easier. These changes, while potentially more impactful than those mentioned previously, are often an easier "sell" because you can highlight the positive benefits for those who are making the changes.

Identifying the benefits or advantages to a change is an important part of any change management exercise. Often a failure to highlight the benefits to someone asked to do something differently is the easiest sign to observe that a change management effort will fail, and it is also the easiest to correct.

Ensuring that before you make any kind of a change (or when you realize a change will be coming), identifying the advantages of the change early will help ensure that you approach the rest of this process with a positive attitude and with answers for people who want to know why the change is occurring and how it will benefit them.

Step 2: Define the Change Initiative

Next, we need to identify the change initiative. This includes more than just the specific change that's needed (which was identified in step 1) and focuses on the entire scope of the change.

The model includes three kinds of individuals who are responsible for change management. These include strategists, implementers, and change recipients.

Strategists are those who identify that something needs to change and what that change should be. In most cases, there are push and pull factors for each change that an organization makes. For example, while Robotic Process Automation (RPA) using MuleSoft may reduce intake workers 2 hours of work a day manually entering paper intakes into their existing system, if the annual price tag is the size of the small organization's budget, they'll be unable to implement it. Deciding on what changes are practical and attainable is part of the strategy effort.

Strategists also do the hard work of thinking about the end state and how they can get there. Depending on the kind of change you are looking for, this work might be done by a chief executive officer (CEO) or chief strategy officer (CSO). If this is purely a technology change, it might be the responsibility of the chief technology officer (CTO). In smaller organizations, a program manager might find themselves responsible for a lot of the change management strategy.

Finally, strategists choose a project sponsor. While this will be explored more in later steps, a project sponsor is someone who will be responsible for shepherding the change down the organizational ladder (and potentially up if the change is coming from lower in the organizational hierarchy).

Change implementers are those who are responsible for implementing the change. In a small organization, the implementer may also be the strategist and potentially even the project sponsor. In a larger organization, these roles may be held by different individuals. In a Salesforce implementation that your organization is doing itself, your implementer is probably your administrator or whoever is responsible for making the configuration changes inside Salesforce.

The goal of the implementers is to make the change as smoothly as possible. The more complex the change, the greater the possibility that the implementation doesn't go smoothly leading to wholesale rejection of the change. Although many times the implementers are the "unsung" heroes, they do play a critical role in ensuring that the change works as intended so that it will be adopted.

Finally, the change recipients are those who are required to interact with the change. In a technology implementation, the change recipients are the end users who will be using the new system. The opinions of the change recipients are very important because they are the customers of the implementers and the strategists and the ones who may have the least influence on the process. They must respect and trust that the change is in their best interest and will provide them with benefits greater than the challenges in adapting their existing behavior.

Step 3: Evaluate the Climate for Change

Once you've identified your change and change management team (or stakeholders), the next step is to look at what environment the change is occurring in. Is there general trust among staff members? Do the existing processes seem to be working for people or are there issues? What have past change management efforts looked like?

It is important to understand the minefield that you might be walking into before you take too many steps. For example, if the organization is low in trust, then it will be hard to convince individuals that this change is really in their best interest. If existing processes are working well and there is not a good rationale for making the change, you will struggle to convince people to do anything. Similarly, if you have had a bad track record of change management attempts in the past, staff will be wary and more skeptical that this latest change will be effective.

This step can be a painful process because it involves acknowledging shortcomings. These may be weaknesses of individuals or departments that otherwise do a great job but simply didn't have the skills or tools (like those discussed here) to ensure that their past change management efforts would be successful. Acknowledging those past mistakes can be important in rebuilding trust.

One source of information on past change management efforts can be employees with long tenure, who may have been around for those changes. Talking to end users about their experiences with past changes can also be valuable because it will give you insight into how they'll approach any future changes. Even the most optimistic of employees can become jaded after multiple failed change management exercises that appear to be dictated from the top with no acknowledgement of the end user's experience. This feedback will help you avoid these common pitfalls.

What's also helpful to assess at this stage is how the change in question is going to affect limited resources. Even small changes require resources to communicate those changes to stakeholders. Examining how proposed changes will affect staff members, funds, training, etc. may help you decide between a few competing courses of action by allowing you to choose the one that has the least impact.

For example, if you know that you need a way for individuals to see clients who have missed their last appointment (already determined by some automation connected to the Appointment object) so that case managers can follow up with them, you may identify a few potential solutions:

1. Do nothing. The current status quo allows case managers to visit the Contact page of each of their clients to see if they have missed appointments.

2. Create a report that allows case managers to see each of the clients assigned to them and whether they missed their last appointment. Share the report with the case managers.

3. Build a Lightning Web Component (LWC) that shows a list of clients missing appointments, and embed it on the case manager's homepage.

Option 1 involves no change in resources, but also no improvement for the case managers. Option 2 requires no custom coding and therefore is less intensive but would require the case managers to understand how to visit the report. Option 3 requires the most resources on the part of the Salesforce team but allows the case managers to quickly see what they need.

If your team had no Apex programmers who could build an LWC, then you are limited to option 2. You might find that needing to go to Reports is minor enough when compared with the difficulty of visiting each Contact page that it is the ideal choice.

Finally, exploring whether the change that is being considered aligns with the organization's strategic plan is valuable. For smaller changes (e.g., updates within the way a program does something), the strategic plan may not be relevant if it acknowledges that the program will continue.

On the other hand, if you plan to transition the case managers to Salesforce but the strategic plan envisions a move of the entire crisis program to ServiceNow, then you may find yourself in significant conflict with senior leaders who are zigging while you are zagging.

Step 4: Develop a Change Plan

Now that you've evaluated the climate that your change is going to take place in and have identified the relevant stakeholders, it is time to build a change plan. This is a comprehensive overview of the change that will take place.

The change management plan should include the specific goals that need to be accomplished for the change to take place. For each of these goals, as many of the steps that can be set out should be. Each action item should be tied to a specific responsible party. You should also ensure that you have checkpoints or gates as opportunities to double check that the plan is being followed.

When Provisio Partners is working through a project, we use a six-step model with two gates:

1. Discovery, where we determine what should change or what we are building

2. Design, where we figure out how best to achieve the desired changes

3. Configuration, where we implement the changes

4. User Acceptance Testing (UAT), where we have users interact with the changes in a sandbox and provide feedback and recommended changes

5. Training, where we introduce all users to the new system or changes

6. Go Live, where we push changes into a production environment and everyone begins to use the system in their day-to-day

The two major gates in this process, shown in Figure 7-1, are at the end of Discovery and the end of User Acceptance Testing.

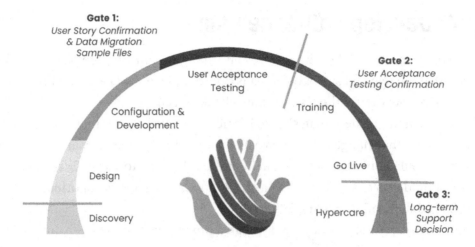

Figure 7-1. *A project implementation process with gates*

At the end of Discovery, we have a set of user stories that set out what the system should do. It's very important to make sure we have enough detail to understand exactly what is desired and in sufficient detail that we can design and then build a solution around this.

Discovery sessions are often led by individuals close to the ground, who are "doing the work" that the changes will affect. Making sure we have the right user stories is helpful in building grassroots support for the changes.

The second major gate is after User Acceptance Testing or UAT. During the UAT phase, trusted users are allowed into the sandbox environment to interact directly with the changes that will be implemented. Their feedback is taken and incorporated into the system before users are trained on it. UAT, then, also represents an opportunity for grassroots support of the changes that will soon be rolling out to everyone.

It's important to clarify the roles that each person will have on the change management team. It's certainly possible for someone who is low level in an organization to play a critical role as a project sponsor, implementer, or even a strategist if they first saw the potential for the change and advocated for their vision.

You should not assume that the highest person in the organization makes the best strategist or implementer, because they may lack the technical skills to implement or the "on the ground" view of the situation to strategize appropriately.

A few tips will help make this process more effective. First, seek out active participants. Rather than assigning individuals duties in this process, you should see who is interested in participating and lean on them first. A disinterested individual can do much harm to a change management process by lowering morale or even actively sabotaging the changes that you are trying to make.

Next, ensure that everyone understands that this is a leadership exercise, not a management one. What that means is that while there is likely to be individuals across the organization involved in this effort, you should avoid "pulling rank." Rather than trying to get individuals to do things by directing them, because you are higher on the org chart than them, instead focus on the benefits to them of achieving these tasks. This is using leadership, rather than management (or personal, rather than positional power.)

Once your plan is created, and it features the goals, action items, roles, and responsibilities of everyone involved, you should examine it to see where you may have been too prescriptive. As Mike Tyson famously said, "Everyone has a plan until they get punched in the mouth." Essentially, your plan cannot be fixed and is unable to change because your organization is not fixed and unable to change.

If there are parts of the plan that you can make more flexible, do so. This may look like only planning a timeline 3 or 6 months out and waiting to see when those activities are complete before scheduling more, or it may look like assigning tasks to a team member temporarily with the understanding that you have others who can fill those roles if it becomes too much for one person.

You may notice that this section has a lack of specifics. Part of that is because the nature of your change management plan will differ depending on the specific thing you are changing. Later in this chapter, you will find a case study example of an organization transitioning to Salesforce that may help fill in some of the gaps that you have.

It is also valuable to consider whether an Agile or a waterfall methodology makes more sense for the project's process. A waterfall model is the traditional software development process where you proceed linearly through the stages we noted previously: discovery, design, configuration, testing, training, and go live. A key part of the waterfall methodology is that there are no changes allowed. You might drop things from the project for time or budget constraints, but you will not really be able to adjust in response to user feedback.

In the Agile methodology, there is a focus on small chunks of development called sprints where you quickly determine what to build, set it up, and then have it looked at. If it needs adjusting, you adjust and then move to the next sprint.

.

There is collaboration and communication throughout that ensures that the project evolves as additional feedback comes in. Provisio Partners uses an Agile methodology to ensure that our implementations can respond to the needs of these end users.

Step 5: Identify a Sponsor

In step 5, you must identify a change management sponsor. Although this activity may have started earlier, here is where it becomes most important. A project sponsor is high enough up in the organization, and trusted enough, that their support helps create a groundswell of support for the changes that you are trying to make.

Ideally, your sponsor will not be the only person to speak positively of the change, but they may be the first person from leadership to do so. This individual should be trusted and seen as a leader but does not necessarily have to be an executive. This means that a respected program manager may be a more effective sponsor of a change to the software used by the case managers who report to them than the CTO who, while much higher in the organization's leadership, has no personal connection to the case managers.

Your sponsor should ideally have a good understanding of the state of the organizational politics that are present and therefore can also assist in identifying others who may be supportive of the changes that you are interested in implementing. In this way, a "snowball" of support may be gained as you move from person to person in furtherance of the change.

A good sponsor will also open doors to you, in that their support can help unstick the glue of bureaucracy that can sometimes make it hard to get things done due to a lack of available resources. The sponsor may also be able to influence changes in a more indirect way. For example, identifying factors important to key stakeholders and ensuring the proposed changes will resolve those difficulties.

Understanding how the project can help your sponsor can also ensure that they are motivated and have a positive influence on the project. For example, knowing that one of the ways the sponsor is evaluated is on the number of clients that their case managers intake. If you can ensure that Salesforce will speed up the data entry process for these intakes, they will be able to draw a clear line between the change to be implemented and an improvement in their own work life.

If you find yourself without a good option for a sponsor, do not despair. A good sponsor may not present themselves immediately. One way to identify potential sponsors and "win them over" is by looking at who will experience the greatest benefit. If this person or people are end users, you can move up the organizational chart until you find someone who has both the political power to assist in changes and potential benefits from the implementation.

After identifying your potential sponsor, make some time for a personal meeting with them to discuss the project. Ensure that you focus primarily on the benefits to the sponsor but also to the others on the organizational chart. Once you have completed this process, you are ready to focus on the recipients of the change: the end users.

Step 6: Prepare the Recipients of Change

Preparing the recipients of the change (shown in Figure 7-2), the end users who will be affected by it, is perhaps the most important and difficult step. Recipients of change are naturally going to be resistant to any change because it disrupts their day-to-day life. This is an unavoidable part of human nature; however, it is not insurmountable.

Figure 7-2. *My cat Pepperoni, an often-unwilling recipient of change*

Focus groups, surveys, and other strategies discussed earlier in this book can be useful ways of understanding how end users will react to these changes. By identifying their pain points, things that they like, and other elements around their day-to-day, you can better prepare them for the changes that are coming.

End users especially are anxious about any change. Providing information can help reduce these feelings. Although you may not be able to let every user of a new system play with it before it launches, providing super users with the opportunity to provide feedback can be very helpful. Recording demos, walkthroughs, and other material can also help.

In Salesforce implementations in particular, it's often very difficult for users to envision how the system works if they've never seen it before. If you can provide demos or recorded sessions, this can help people understand how the new system will help improve their day-to-day.

Part of how well your end users accept the change is based on how well you have understood their needs. If you are going through an external consultancy, this means how well the discovery process went. If this is an internal change management effort, there may not be a formal discovery process, but there is still a need to understand the end user's concerns and adequately address their pain points.

Proactively reaching out to those individuals who may represent a bigger threat to the adoption can also help by winning them over. This could be end users who have had bad experiences with change management in the past, highly placed individuals in the organization who can stop the change effort from happening, or others who you feel may have an influence on the team.

Although most of this change management process focuses on the end users, they are not the only recipients of change. Even individuals who are not using the system are still affected by it, so you should not neglect to consider the impact on senior leaders, accountants, and others who are peripherally affected by the change.

Step 7: Create the Cultural Fit

An organization's culture represents the beliefs, values, and institutional knowledge that guide the team members. Every organization has a culture, though it may be hard to see if you've been working in your organization for a while. This culture is the lens through which all actions are seen.

Culture can explain things as wide-ranging as whether you can call up your boss's boss to discuss a situation, whether having a drink at 5 p.m. is looked down upon, or whether you are expected or even required to take your vacation or if doing so is damaging to your career.

Understanding your organization's culture is key to making changes happen effectively. By ensuring the change follows the unwritten changes of the organization, you increase the likelihood that the change is accepted. While there's no easy way to tell what cultural values apply to your organization, activities like focus groups can also help you ensure that you are not inadvertently trampling on organizational norms.

If your organization is very hierarchical, you will want to make sure that you respect the chain of command and involve individuals at high levels of the organization so they feel included in the process. If your organization prefers to have plans approved by multiple layers of management, ensure that you present it early and seek out the relevant approvals before you proceed.

Some organizations highly value transparency, and stakeholders will be suspicious if you don't provide them with detailed and regular updates as the implementation process proceeds. Others value confidentiality more than transparency and would prefer that you only "read in" those who have an absolute need to know so that they can carefully orchestrate the communication around the changes.

These are ways of reducing the organizational conflict that can result if you don't keep your organization's values in mind before you begin trying to make changes.

Step 8: Develop and Choose a Change Leader Team

A change leader is the person who sets out the vision for the change. In step 5, you identified a project sponsor. The sponsor is the person who provides support and motivation to the project and helps ensure its success. The change leader may be the sponsor or they may be distinct, but their role is to ensure that everyone understands the goals of the change and can help marshal support for the changes.

Around the change leader are other individuals who make up the change team. These individuals will be the strategists and implementers who will be pursuing this project. It's important to assess the qualifications of the team and ensure that you have everything that you need to be successful. For example, if you are changing CRM systems and moving from ServiceNow to Salesforce, you may find that you lack the Salesforce knowledge needed. This could be resolved by adding an experienced consulting firm or by individuals pursuing training in the platform as soon as they become aware that this knowledge will be needed.

Another area that is commonly lacking in Salesforce implementations specifically is data migration experience. This is a specialized area that is of particular interest to implementers of new Salesforce organizations who work in evaluation, impact, or outcomes because high-quality data is the backbone of this work. By ensuring that you have the resources you need to perform high-quality data migration (or bringing resources that do onto the team), you will be better prepared to handle the transition.

Once you've assembled your team, you should clarify their roles to make sure that everyone knows which role they are playing. Your implementers should know they are implementers, and your strategists should know they are strategists. If there is too much role diffusion, people on the team may not know who to turn to for decisions or how they are best able to contribute.

Step 9: Create Small Wins for Motivation

Change management efforts can sometimes take a long time to come to fruition. Small or medium-sized projects may take 6 or 12 months. Larger efforts may take years. Throughout all this process, it can be hard to keep people motivated that the result will be worth the effort that it takes to get there. This is where the process of small wins comes in handy.

These small wins are incremental steps that can help encourage individuals to keep participating in the process if they are a team member, to keep supporting the project if they are more tangentially connected such as a UAT tester, and to avoid actively badmouthing the project if they are a "spectator" on the sidelines.

Small wins will look different throughout the change management process. Early on, the win may be the participation of individuals who are curious about the changes and interested in providing their input.

Later in the process, being able to see their feedback reflected in the next deliverables such as the design or demos of configured functionality may be the small wins. If you already use Salesforce and are making large updates, you may find yourself able to deploy smaller parts of the project in phases.

"Shout-outs" or public thank yous to the individuals involved can also help keep them motivated during what is often a thankless process. Celebrating small wins also has the benefit of keeping the process front of mind, which can help prevent resources being diverted from the project in a way that can lead to its failure by virtue of not being finished before it gets launched.

Sometimes organizations will be reluctant to celebrate small wins because they feel like it dilutes the impact of the "big wins." This couldn't be further from the truth. Instead, small wins keep the motivation up so that the big wins can be appreciated by everyone who understands just how long a process it was to go from the old state to the new one. Celebrate those wins to keep the momentum going.

Step 10: Constantly and Strategically Communicate the Change

One of the most common criticisms of change efforts is that they come from the top without any consultation. Waking up one day to find out that the way that you are going to do your job going forward is changing radically is uncomfortable at best. Change creates anxiety, even if it is anticipated as a positive change (if you don't believe me, think back to the butterflies you felt when starting a new job!)

The way that you avoid this pitfall is to ensure that you are communicating the changes to the people who will be asked to them on. The more involved, aware, and participatory the process feels, the less automatic resistance to change you'll experience.

One example of a positive communication effort I am familiar with included a dashboard on the homepage that tracked the rollout of updates to their Salesforce organization. As the project hit major milestones, the dashboard was updated so that everyone could see what the upcoming goals were and when they would be accessible to end users. This helped keep everyone in the loop and prevent confusion.

Other options to communicate change include weekly team meetings, quarterly department updates, emails, or newsletters, as shown in Figure 7-3. Any existing method that your organization uses to communicate with stakeholders can be used to ensure that knowledge of the change management effort is distributed.

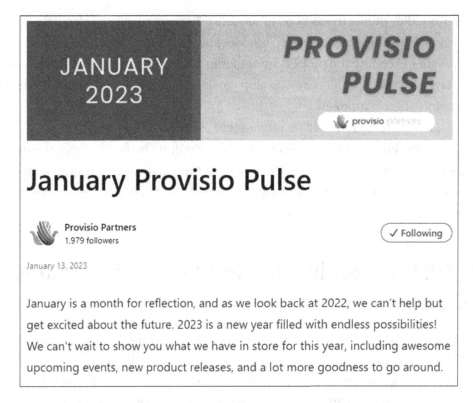

Figure 7-3. A newsletter as an example of strategic communication

When we discuss strategically communicating the change, what is meant is ensuring that you focus on what to communicate and when. If you overshare, you risk desensitizing individuals to the communication because they get so many of them that are of no or low importance. On the other hand, if you choose to share too infrequently, you will find that individuals are left in the dark.

The right cadence will depend on the size of the project, the estimated impact, and the length of time planned for it. The larger the project and the expected impact, the more frequent the communication. The longer the planned project, the more important regular updates are.

Sometimes there is opposition to regular communication because people believe that this will open them up to project-damaging criticism. It's a reasonable thought, but one that I disagrees with. If you do find the project getting criticized, rather than shying away from that, you should take it as an opportunity to directly engage those individuals and work to resolve their criticisms.

What sometimes appears to be a wholesale rejection of a platform or project can sometimes boil down to a dislike of a small part that is in fact changeable.

Even if their change is an objection to the entire technology platform, there are likely benefits for the individual who is upset that can be elucidated with careful questioning. This can help turn an outspoken critic into a quiet supporter, if not an advocate.

Step 11: Measure Progress of the Change Effort

While the change management process is in progress, it is important to measure the progress of the change effort. This will take many forms depending on the specific changes that you are introducing.

When I was training crisis line workers, a pretest and posttest were used. Questions focused on the trainee's attitudes toward people with mental health issues, their beliefs about suicide and suicidal ideation, and knowledge questions about how to handle individuals in crisis. During the pretest, we knew that most of our trainees did not know how to handle these situations, and so we recognized they would not score very highly based on what the desired responses were.

After the training, we administered an identical assessment and found, consistently, that their knowledge, beliefs, and attitudes had shifted in the direction that we wanted so that they had the right understanding and behavior to be an effective crisis worker. This is one example of how we measured a change management effort.

If you are introducing a new or updated Salesforce implementation, you may find the User Adoption Dashboards by Salesforce Labs helpful, shown in Figure 7-4. These are a set of dashboards that measure key performance indicators (KPIs) around user login history, new records created, and use of certain features like Activities (Tasks, Events, and Emails). These dashboards can be put on the homepage for all users to use or used by monitors of the change management effort higher in the organization.

Figure 7-4. *A User Adoption Dashboard running in a sandbox*

Focus groups, town halls, office hours, or other forms of open communication can also help you monitor the progress of the change effort by allowing you to talk directly to the people who are supposed to be using the system to find out what their needs are. Sometimes something small can be a big barrier to someone who is not tech savvy or is already wary of the project, and so getting this feedback (and acting on it!) can play a major role in ensuring that people continue to follow the changes that are being implemented.

Step 12: Integrate Lessons Learned

The final step to the change management process is to integrate the lessons learned into the next change management effort. This is often overlooked in the rush to celebrate a positive launch or hastily done after a bad launch.

It's important that you explore what worked and what didn't, because each organization will have specific things that work effectively well (or not), and each change management process will be influenced by the unique situations present at the time.

For example, I participated in an implementation featuring a large amount of turnover with the staff whose technology platform we were building. As a result of the turnover, we knew more about the original intended use of certain features and functions than the staff members did. This made for a difficult implementation when new staff were confused about why design decisions were made, until we were able to meet with those staff and clarify the design.

A Case Study of Change Management

Change management is an ongoing process, but hopefully you have learned more about the process and are better prepared to engage in change management in your organizations. What follows is a brief example of how each of the change management processes could apply to an organization that has an active Salesforce organization but has decided to implement some new impact measurement and outcome evaluations tools.

This fictional organization called SPARKLES (the Southern Pennsylvania Referral, Knowledge and Legal Education Services) is a legal aid organization that provides assistance to individuals in Pennsylvania via a helpline that allows them to get legal support.

While the organization's lawyers do not represent clients, they can advise individuals of legal issues and provide advice throughout the lifecycle of their cases and refer them to attorneys who can represent them formally.

Determine the Idea and Its Context

The primary change will be in the intake and assessment processes. Currently, the organization takes calls which they record in Salesforce as Cases. When someone calls back, they go back to the original Case and record Case Updates, which is a child object of the Case. All details of the legal issue are recorded in the narrative sections on the Case, which limits the ability of the organization to understand the impact of their work on their clients.

Instead, the organization would like to move to a standardized intake that collects the same information from every client including their level of distress, the kind of legal issue they have, and how long they have been dealing with it.

Define the Change Initiative

In this step, we need to identify who the strategists, integrators, and change recipients are. In this case, it is the Director of Measurement and Evaluation (M&E) who has been with the organization for 5 years who is the strategist.

They have hired a consulting firm to implement the changes they need and added a project team comprised of the program manager of the call center and two attorney-call takers to represent SPARKLES. This project team, plus the consulting firm, will make up the implementers.

Evaluate the Climate for Change

SPARKLES has had bad luck with technology systems in the past. Many of their staff have used a variety of technology systems before, none of which have lasted very long. They are very comfortable with paper but have adjusted to Salesforce.

The Director of M&E who is leading the change management efforts is respected, though somewhat distanced from the day-to-day work of the lawyers. The legal director who oversees the attorneys is uncertain about the advantages and would prefer their system not to be changed.

Develop a Change Plan

Now that we have the information we need, we can develop our change plan, shown in Table 7-1. We identify the following goals and action items. This is a trimmed-down list; the real one would likely be longer.

Table 7-1. *A sample change management plan*

Goal/action item	Timeline	Responsible party
Develop a new intake form	1 month	Legal Department/IT Department
Choose or create an assessment	1 month	Head of Legal Department
Focus group the assessment and intake form	1 month	Director of Measurement and Evaluation
Decide who should be administered the assessment	1 month	Director of Measurement and Evaluation
Soft launch the assessment to a group of trusted users	3 months	IT Department
Tweak things in response to feedback	2 months	Director of Measurement and Evaluation
Roll it out to everyone	1 month	IT Department
Make it mandatory to submit a case	3 months	IT Department

From start to finish, this process is estimated to take 13 months. The Legal Department, who oversees the lawyers, is responsible for deciding on the format of the assessment and intake, while IT handles the rollout of the changes. Most other items are the responsibility of the Director of Measurement and Evaluation who is spearheading these changes.

Although the timeline appears to fit a waterfall methodology, the likelihood of on-the-fly changes and quick fixes means that this is going to be closer to an agile implementation.

Identify a Sponsor

Now it is time to identify a sponsor of the project. While the director of M&E is the driving force behind the changes, the legal director is the supervisor of the attorneys who will bear the brunt of the changes. For this reason, they are an obvious choice to act as a project sponsor if they can be convinced to come along with the project.

The director of M&E has decided to book a meeting with the legal director and talk to them about the project. During the conversation, the director of M&E can explain some of the benefits to the attorneys and how moving to an intake and assessment form will cut down on the narrative typing the attorneys they need to do. This will both improve the data quality of the organization and reduce the typing and time it takes to take each call.

Prepare the Recipients of Change

With the Legal Department director on board, it is time to prepare the attorneys. It will be 4 months from the start of the project before they see the new assessment and intake form in a soft launch. In that time, it is helpful to let attorneys know that this is coming.

By highlighting the reduction in the amount of typing that the lawyers will need to do, you may help encourage them to look forward to the changes. Also, knowing that they will get to provide input and change the intake and assessment to make it most useful for them will also help build their excitement.

Create the Cultural Fit

As mentioned earlier, the organization hasn't had the best luck with technology platforms. The lawyers are wary of change, and the legal director doesn't want to make things more difficult for their staff than they need to.

The organization has a relatively flat structure with open communication; however, the lawyers are more insulated than the other parts of the organization due to their unique role in the service provision. This means that when it comes to feedback, it will most likely be communicated to the legal director first.

One positive of this organization's culture is their appreciation of cats, like my cat shown in Figure 7-5.

Figure 7-5. *My third cat*

Develop and Choose a Change Leader Team

As the change management plan notes, there are a few key change team members. These include the director of M&E, the IT Department, and the director of the Legal Department. These team members are best positioned to build support and ensure that the implementation of the changes goes smoothly.

Create Small Wins for Motivation

Small wins in this project that will be important to highlight include the approval of the draft intake and assessment form, the soft launch, and the improvements made. Collecting data during the soft launch will be especially important.

If you can highlight to the team that the attorneys who soft-launched the new tools saw their Average Handle Time (AHT) drop from 20 minutes to 12 minutes because they had to do much less typing, it will help encourage others to follow along.

Constantly and Strategically Communicate the Change

Another use of the change management plan is to guide the communication efforts. Each of the items in the change management plan may be associated with a specific communication, for example, inviting individuals to the focus group to evaluate the new assessment and intake form.

When the soft launch occurs, letting others know that it's coming can help build excitement and ensure individuals are giving feedback.

Measure Progress of the Change Effort

To measure the progress of the change effort, a report that shows the number of intakes and assessments would be valuable. If you can see the attorneys using the tools that have been created, that will help you know they are being adopted.

Additionally, monitoring the average call time and watching it decline as the attorneys get better at using the intake and assessment will also help. Finally, allowing open-ended feedback and continuing to incorporate the recommendations into the system will help give people a sense of ownership.

Integrate Lessons Learned

At the end of the change management process, you can integrate your lessons learned into the next change management effort that you undertake. Good work SPARKLES! You have shepherded your organization through a challenging change, successfully.

Conclusion

Hopefully you have come away from this chapter with a better understanding of the change management process and how you can implement it in your own organization. There are many theories of change management, and you may find that you prefer some frameworks or processes over others.

Don't be afraid to experiment and even build an eclectic framework of your own development that considers your organization's unique quirks. Good luck!

CHAPTER 8

Case Studies

In this chapter, we will review all the frameworks and processes discussed to date in three case studies. These case studies represent fictional organizations based on real ones that I have worked at or consulted for and will help illustrate the concepts by taking the theoretical and incorporating some of the real issues that can make impact measurement and outcome evaluation more difficult than it can seem at first glance.

Each of these organizations has its own quirks, and so the impact measurement and outcome techniques that apply in one do not necessarily translate to another.

Case Study 1: Nonprofit Crisis Line

In this first case study, we will look at the impact measurement processes at a nonprofit crisis line. Nonprofit crisis lines have many of the qualities that nonprofits will recognize: volunteer-supported, limited budgets, and a critical mission to the public.

Introduction to the Organization

The Distress Center of Fort Bend is a small, volunteer-supported crisis line. Located in a county with a population of 700,000, they represent the first call for many people who are in distress, dealing with a crisis, or who are suicidal. The organization is a 501(c)(3), so donations are tax deductible. Founded in 1970, the crisis line is the only 24/7 mental health line in the region.

The organization is primarily funded by a Community Foundation, who provides 60% of the operating budget which represents about $200,000. The remaining 40% of the budget ($133,000) is raised from several fundraising events, one-off grants, and donations.

© Dustin MacDonald 2023
D. MacDonald, *Impact Measurement and Outcomes Evaluation Using Salesforce for Nonprofits*,
https://doi.org/10.1007/978-1-4842-9708-7_8

These fundraisers include a Suicide Awareness Walk, an event called Martini Manicure where women can enjoy a martini and a manicure sponsored by local businesses, and Cookies and Crisis, where people can buy cookies and other baked goods with the proceeds going to the organization.

Office expenses represent about $40,000 a year. This includes office supplies, rent of the building, security expenditures, and professional services like accounting.

There are four staff members whose combined salaries equal $200,000. These include an executive director making $75,000, a helpline program manager who makes $50,000, a fundraising director who makes $40,000 and a support group coordinator who makes $35,000. Additional expenditures include summer interns who are hired to provide additional support to the program manager.

Most of the actual call-taking is handled by volunteers. Each volunteer receives 40 hours of training in emotional support, crisis intervention, suicide risk assessment, and other topics so that they are prepared to take calls. This includes classroom theory, role-plays and practice exercises, and time on the phone supervised by an experienced crisis worker.

The motivation for the current upgrade is that funding from the primary funder has been decreasing over time. This has caused the amount that needs to be raised by fundraising to increase year over year. During the COVID-19 pandemic, the Community Foundation explained that given their drop in donations, they may be unable to support the organization going forward.

Current Technology

The crisis line currently uses an Access database as their primary call-taking software called CAOS (Crisis Access-based Operating System). This system suffers from a number of major shortcomings.

First, because it is stored locally, you can only access information when you are physically in the crisis line building. Second, it has a number of bugs due to its homegrown nature. Third, it is difficult to search the database for information. Finally, there is no reporting capability.

Calls come in on a POTS (Plain Old Telephone Service) line with no ability to track them. This is the same technology that was available in 1970.

These issues have limited the organization's ability to demonstrate the value of the crisis line and pursue strategic growth opportunities. In the next 5 years, the organization would like to expand their catchment area to a neighboring area which has very limited helpline coverage and increase services to college students.

Both strategic expansion processes will require a data-driven approach to ensure that funders are willing to support these initiatives.

Planned Technology

After engaging in a Request for Proposal (RFP) process, the crisis line has decided to adopt Salesforce and the Nonprofit Cloud. A few factors helped sell Salesforce over the other vendors: the flexibility of the Salesforce platform means that it can be customized in the future as the organization's needs change.

Some of the vendors sold software that was not web-based. The existing limitations of the Access solution they use today were clear, and so a Cloud-based solution made the most sense. This would allow staff to work from multiple locations and automation to be built that could prepare records for approval, send emails as needed, and so on.

Additionally, Salesforce is not helpline specific. Some of the vendors the organization looked at are crisis line specific, which was great for that specific program but meant that they would need to adopt a new software package if they were to grow beyond their existing services.

Finally, the Nonprofit Success Pack (NPSP) provides the organization with a built-in fundraising platform. Given that existing fundraising and development efforts were managed in Excel spreadsheets, this was a major value add that met a need the organization wasn't even anticipating.

In addition to adopting Salesforce as the primary technology platform, the organization also adopted a new Cloud-based telephone system that would allow them to engage in call tracking. This will enable the calculation of real call center metrics for the first time like Average Handle Time (AHT), After Call Work (ACW), Average Talk Time (ATT), and the wait time before a caller in crisis is connected to a crisis worker.

Old Data Model

The CAOS Access Database is very simple. Each person who calls in is created as a Caller record. Each call that comes in is created as a Call record. There are narrative and picklist/drop-down options to provide information such as the kind of call, the call resolution, and the beginning and end time of the call.

One of the current frustrations with the system is that if the crisis worker forgets to record the start and end time of the call, they must rely on their memory. This means that the call time records are frequently inaccurate.

Another issue is that the system makes frequent use of modal dialogs, limiting your ability to visit multiple screens at once. Salesforce eliminates this with a tab-based structure that allows you to quickly switch between multiple records at once.

New Data Model

Working with a consultant, the choice was made to implement Nonprofit Cloud with Amazon Voice and Salesforce Service Cloud Voice. Each call that comes in will be a Voice Call. This voice call record will store all information about the phone call itself.

Attached to that Voice Call will be a Crisis Call record. The Crisis Call object will store information about the type of crisis, the response provided by the crisis worker and the outputs and disposition of the call.

A Salesforce Screen Flow automatically creates a Crisis Call object when the Voice Call object is created and guides the crisis worker through providing the information necessary.

Additionally, the Case object will be used to record referrals that are made to community agencies during the call.

Impact and Outcome

The crisis line has a number of choices to make to demonstrate their value. They decide to use Salesforce Reports and Dashboards to give staff access to the information that they need to do their jobs better.

To demonstrate the importance of the crisis line to the community, they opt for a social return on investment (SROI) analysis. This will allow them to approach funders, in particular the local government, for funding by showing how much money they save the county by reducing police and ambulance requests.

Additionally, the organization decides to implement standardized assessments to track the level of distress among callers at the start and end of the period.

Reports and Dashboards

Reports and Dashboards are a logical first choice for building new insights. By creating a report on the Voice Call object, the staff can gain an insight into the average call time.

By adding a declarative lookup rollup summary field for the number of calls on the Contact object, they can run a report on this object to see which individuals are calling most frequently.

Because the Call Response object includes the Type of Call, checkboxes for the crisis worker to indicate the responses they made (such as active listening, problem solving, or active crisis rescue), and the reactions from the caller (decrease in distress, increased coping skills, and immediate safety secured), reports can be created to allow them to demonstrate which responses are most common and who is the "average" person reaching out for support.

Social Return on Investment

The SROI process, detailed more fully in Chapter 2, allows you to take the tangible outputs that you can recognize from a situation such as a reduction in distress during a call and translate that into a longer-term outcome which is something that is socially valuable and harder to quantify.

The SROI process is ideal for a crisis line environment because in the moment, the crisis workers provide a lot of support and prevent the need for emergency responses, with a team of trained volunteers whose expenses to maintain are much less than those emergency responders.

By completing an SROI analysis like the one demonstrated in Chapter 2, the crisis line learns that for each dollar invested in the crisis line, they generate $4 in social value.

The largest source of that social value comes from active rescues that prevent a suicide death and high-risk crisis interventions that occur before someone needs an ambulance. By sending them in a taxi, you reduce the need to send paramedics but still get the individual to a safe place in the moment of the crisis.

Assessments

One of the biggest changes that the organization is planning to make is their assessment process. Currently, they use a paper-based suicide risk assessment tool. They've decided to move to a computerized version of this tool and add additional items.

By using a Dynamic Lightning Page, they can set the criteria for each item on the page. When the call taker goes to create a new Suicide Risk Assessment record, they can begin making their choices on the assessment tool.

The tool dynamically scores the assessment and presents them with additional information on how to respond. This ensures they provide the best assessment possible and they ask the right questions.

In addition to computerizing the suicide risk assessment, they are also going to take advantage of the new digital phone system to automatically prompt individuals at the beginning of the call to rate their level of distress from 1 to 5. This will allow the crisis line to assess their level of distress at the end of the call, to improve their call-taking.

Surveys

One of the main services the organization provides outside of the crisis line is suicide and homicide survivor support groups. These support groups are for individuals who have lost someone in their life to suicide death or to homicide.

Many of these individuals first learned about these groups by calling the crisis line, and many of them have used the crisis line throughout their grief journey. For this reason, they are ideal candidates for surveys that will help improve the organization's services.

A short, four-question survey is developed and given anonymously to people who have completed the 8-week survivor groups. The four questions are as follows:

1. What would you prefer that we change about the program?

2. Are there any services we don't offer that you think we should?

3. Do you have any other feedback for us?

4. Please rate your trust in the organization on a scale of 1-10.

These questions, except for the last one, are all open-ended, free response questions. This will ensure that we do not constrain the answers before we understand the community's opinion of the crisis line. The reason for the focus on trust is to understand what the community receptions of the programs are.

Change Management Process

The change management process needed to be handled carefully. The new system was trialed and implemented over a 6-month period. During that time, most users would continue to use the old system, while some would start to use the new one. Once the new system was up and running, training sessions were held to ensure that each crisis worker could work with the system.

Once the system went live, office hours allowed staff to ask questions and submit change requests, and the system was tweaked to ensure that the system was responsive to the crisis workers' needs.

Final Outcomes

The end result of this process is a Salesforce system that allows crisis workers to easily and quickly take calls, that allows staff to report out on the impact their crisis workers are having, manage the contacts in the system and expand in the future.

Case Study 2: Chamber of Commerce

In our second case study, we examine a Chamber of Commerce. These nonprofit organizations are often closely involved in economic development and play a crucial role in powering the economic engines of many communities.

Introduction to the Organization

The Chamber is a 501(c)(6) Chamber of Commerce in a suburban area. This Chamber has as its mission to increase the number of businesses in the region, to create more jobs, and to promote a positive climate to do business in.

The organization currently uses spreadsheets and paper for most of its work. This includes contacts with businesses, managing a revolving loan fund, selling property on an Industrial Park, and a limited amount of lobbying.

Until the adoption of Salesforce, this required huge amounts of mental labor and a lot of paper to manage. It was decided to move to Salesforce to meet the goals of the new strategic plan which included selling 20% of the Industrial Park, adding five new businesses within the next five bills, and building relationships with legislators.

One of the reasons to choose Salesforce is because of Net Zero Cloud, which will allow the organization to pursue net-zero carbon emissions. As a Chamber of Commerce representing businesses, they would like to demonstrate the importance of net zero.

By modeling how you can track and reduce your emissions, they hope to encourage businesses to follow suit. Additionally, there are a number of funding opportunities that are available for companies willing to pursue net zero that the Chamber would assist those businesses in applying for once they are ready to pursue net-zero emissions.

Current Technology

The current technology includes Excel spreadsheets and paper. This is the same technology the organization has used for years. The Revolving Loan Fund is managed primarily on paper, while information about the various projects the Chamber undertakes are managed with a series of spreadsheets used as project management tracking documents.

Although there is a website, it has limited functionality. IT does include a database of local businesses and other information but allows for minimal interaction by the public. This makes it hard for people to stay involved in the work of the organization and has led to lots of information being distributed on Facebook instead.

Planned Technology

After engaging a consultant to choose a new platform, the Chamber has decided to adopt Salesforce. Salesforce makes a good candidate for the Chamber for several reasons. One, it will give them the opportunity to think deliberately about what kind of data they want to store and where it should live in the system, given the flexibility of the Salesforce CRM.

Two, an unauthenticated Experience Cloud will make a good replacement for the website because it can be maintained merely by updating the Salesforce records in the background. This will cut down on the work of maintaining both a website and a separate CRM.

Finally, automation will help with a variety of administrative tasks around renewals, reaching out to businesses, and other regular tasks that the administration does. This will free up the staff for more strategic actions like identifying new business opportunities for the community, pursuing loans through the Revolving Loan Fund, and other more intensive activities.

Old Data Model

One spreadsheet has each of the business's members along with basic information about when they joined the Chamber, how much their membership is and how often they are billed, and contact information for the CEO or other leadership.

Another spreadsheet is used to record the last contact time of each business. As the staff call the business owner, they update the spreadsheet with the description of the contact. This helps them avoid calling the same person repeatedly for the same reason while neglecting other members.

A third spreadsheet is used to track potential new members. These include new businesses that have come to town, past businesses that have not yet joined the Chamber.

A final spreadsheet is used to track the Revolving Loan Fund details. This includes how much the loan was made for, what the term is, when the last payment was made, and so on. This helps the staff keep track of the checks they receive monthly from the organizations that have received RLF loans and are making their payments.

New Data Model

The new data model replicates all the existing components while gaining new features and functionality based on Salesforce. By using the Contact object to track the individual contacts and the Account object to track the organizations, the first two spreadsheets will be replaced.

Using the Activities that come out of the box with Salesforce (Tasks and Events), the Chamber can know when they've contacted each person and each organization.

Additionally, using Account Contact Roles, they can go beyond just storing the CEO, but each person at the business that they have contact with. This can include someone responsible for renewing the membership and other frontline employees who they may wish to survey to find out how they can make the Chamber more useful to them.

Potential members will be added into Salesforce as Accounts, but a custom field called Membership_Status__c will be used to track whether they have joined the Chamber or not. By using the status of "Potential/Non-Member," they can create List Views to filter the list of accounts just for those who are not in the Chamber. This ensures the third spreadsheet of potential members is unnecessary.

The final spreadsheet is the Revolving Loan Fund details. This will be tracked using a custom object called Revolving_Loan_Fund__c. This Revolving Loan Fund object will store all the information about the loans that have been issued and their current status. Additionally, by adding a Loan Payment object as a Master-Detail object to the Revolving Loan Fund object, each payment can also be recorded.

Impact and Outcome

A number of technologies and methodologies will be used to ensure a strong impact and good outcomes.

Interviews

The Chamber decides to interview several longstanding members to ask them what keeps them participating in the Chamber. This will help guide the Chamber as they come up with a new strategic plan.

Based on the interviews they conducted, the Chamber determined that what members value is the access to technical assistance and information. The Chamber decides to add Business Plan Assistance, start a new business book library, and start "office hours" where individuals with business problems can discuss them with the Chamber.

Einstein Prediction Builder

Based on the information that was collected on the past members of the Chamber, Einstein Prediction Builder will be used to create a numeric prediction of the likelihood that a new organization will join the Chamber. This will help the staff improve their outreach to these organizations by understanding what factors contribute to someone joining the Chamber and to focus their efforts on the companies most likely to sign up for membership.

Einstein Next Best Action (NBA) can also be utilized by the Chamber in those situations where someone is interested in canceling their membership. There may be opportunities to salvage that membership by downgrading them to a lower membership tier or offering them some other benefits that they may not be aware of.

Flows and Automation

As mentioned previously, automation will be used to ensure regular contact with businesses. Based on the Last Contact Date on the Account object (representing the Business), a Flow will create a notification for the staff member assigned to that business to reach out to them.

When Revolving Loan Payments are due, they will be entered into Salesforce once they are received. If a payment is more than 5 days overdue, an email will be sent to the staff member assigned to that business, as well as to the primary contact reminding them to submit their payment.

Experience Cloud

An unauthenticated Experience Cloud has been created to replace the old Chamber website. While most of the content on the website is static, one of the major changes is that visitors can now browse the Account records in Salesforce for current members. This allows them to see selected information about a member of the Chamber such as when they joined the Chamber, what kind of services they provide, and contact details for them.

This Experience Cloud is easy enough for nontechnical staff to maintain, in contrast to the existing website which requires knowledge of HTML and other web scripting languages.

Additionally, the Chamber is considering adopting an authenticated user experience in the future, to allow Chamber members to log in and update their own details without needing to involve staff at all, further freeing them up to pursue more strategic goals.

Final Outcomes

The result of this Salesforce implementation is that the Chamber of Commerce can now manage all their data inside a single and concentrate on the strategic and high-level activities that require their economic development knowledge, rather than on basic administration and data management.

Case Study 3: Homeless Shelter and Food Pantry

Our final case study in this chapter is a homeless shelter and food pantry. These organizations provide services to some of the most vulnerable in our communities, and often with very limited resources and an overwhelming demand.

Introduction to the Organization

The Downtown Mission is a homeless shelter and food pantry that serves 400 residents every day. Services include shelter beds, showers, laundry, medical care, counseling, access to fax machines, mail, legal support, career services, and more.

In addition to the dedicated shelter that provides three meals a day, the Mission also provides access to drop-in services for individuals who are housed but living in extreme poverty. This includes dozens of people who use the food pantry each day.

Current Technology

The organization currently provides services with a mix of technology platforms. They manage the shelter beds using the Homeless Management Information Systems (HMIS) dictated by the county, along with the MissionTracker software system.

The food pantry is managed with Food Pantry Helper. Medical services are recorded in the Epic electronic health record (EHR) system. Mental health services, legal support, and career services are tracked in yet another CRM database.

This decision to adopt Salesforce is to bring all these systems under one roof and solve the issue of detached reporting and data management issues that come with each system having their own requirements.

Planned Technology

Salesforce will be used as the all-in-one data management solution. Integrations will be used with Epic and HMIS to allow information from Salesforce to be pushed to these systems. Because of the nature of federal homelessness funding, these systems cannot be removed, but they can be integrated.

A custom homelessness solution will be implemented to allow shelter bed management, and Nonprofit Cloud Case Management (NCCM) will be used to track each client and what programs and services they are receiving from the shelter.

Other custom solutions include the use of a barcode scanner to scan people in and out of the shelter for the purpose of tracking visitors and DocuSign (which integrates nicely with Salesforce) for the signing of consent forms.

Old Data Model

The old data model involved a variety of systems, each with different databases and ways of storing information. For that reason, it makes more sense to focus on the new data model and how Salesforce will help bring all this information together.

New Data Model

Both shelter and food pantry visitors will be in the system as Contacts, while the Household model in NCCM (where Accounts are used to track the household members) will be used.

Shelter visits will be recorded as a record of the Service Delivery, as will each of the other services that they receive including legal support, medical support, counseling, and so on. When a guest is scanned into the shelter, a record of a custom object called Shelter Visit will be created so that their entry and exit times can be recorded. This will allow the shelter to keep a running list of who is currently in the shelter.

When guests are new to the shelter, they are required to complete the Vulnerability Index - Service Prioritization Decision Assistance Tool. This tool allows their risk to be prioritized so that they can determine their eligibility for services across the county.

Consent forms will be integrated with DocuSign and populate a custom Consent Form object. This will be Master-Detail to the Program Engagement object so that you can keep track of how many consent forms each guest has completed.

Impact and Outcome

From here, we can begin to look at ways to determine the impact and the outcome at this organization.

Pre-Post Comparison

During the intake, the VI-SPDAT is completed for guests who will be staying in the shelter. All other service recipients will complete the Arizona Self Sufficiency Matrix (ASSM). This will allow staff to understand the change in the visitor's ability to cope as they proceed through the program.

By putting the ASSM scores onto a dashboard, each Case Manager can see the scores of their clients over time to understand if they are increasing or decreasing.

Interviews

As each guest prepares to leave the shelter and move into permanent housing, they are interviewed by a staff member to find out what could improve the shelter experience. These notes are then incorporated into a continuous improvement process to ensure that the experience of the clients is the best that it can be.

Final Outcomes

The ultimate result of the Salesforce implementation is a system that brings all the organization's data under one roof.

Conclusion

As you can see, each organization comes to do the work of impact measurement and outcome evaluation from a different place. Each has different strengths and weaknesses and as a result has different outcome evaluations and impact measurement techniques available to them.

Look to these as examples that hopefully inspire your own work as you proceed through the remainder of this book.

CHAPTER 9

Advanced Techniques

In this chapter, we look at some advanced techniques for impact measurement and outcome evaluation. These techniques go beyond base Salesforce and Nonprofit Cloud functionality to tap into Salesforce's advanced artificial intelligence and machine learning offerings called Einstein.

We will learn how to use Experience Cloud to get data from constituents and insert it right into your Salesforce database without you needing to do anything to it, and we will examine some AppExchange solutions that go beyond what Salesforce provides to allow you to better model outcomes.

What Is Einstein?

Einstein is the name of the platform that Salesforce uses to do artificial intelligence and machine learning. It compromises a wide variety of products including the following:

Einstein Next Best Action (NBA)

Einstein Next Best Action allows you to respond dynamically to situations that affect individuals whose records you are working with in Salesforce. The easiest example to understand is a situation like calling in to your cable company. If you tell the Customer Service Representative (CSR) that you want to cancel your cable, they can click a button on their screen for customers who want to cancel.

When they do that, Einstein NBA jumps into action. It can use code, including Einstein Prediction Builder (discussed later) or a set of decision rules created by the person populating the tool, to tell the CSR exactly what to do next.

You can see Einstein Next Best Action's Strategy Builder in Figure 9-1.

© Dustin MacDonald 2023
D. MacDonald, *Impact Measurement and Outcomes Evaluation Using Salesforce for Nonprofits*,
https://doi.org/10.1007/978-1-4842-9708-7_9

Figure 9-1. *The Einstein Strategy Builder showing different elements that can be used to create a strategy to generate recommendations*

Einstein Prediction Builder may know that individuals with profiles like this caller who call in and cancel are much less likely to cancel if you offer them a 50% discount for one year. I had this experience when cancelling a *New York Times* subscription because it was going from $4 a month to $4 a week. They offered to keep me at the cheaper subscription rate, and so I did not cancel. This is an example of the kind of advantage Einstein NBA can offer.

Returning to the cable cancellation example, Einstein tells the CSR to offer you a 20% discount because this is the best way to keep your business. He offers you the discount. Now, there is a decision tree. The decision tree includes two buttons. Either the customer decided not to cancel (great!), or the customer continues to want to cancel.

If you click that the customer decided not to cancel, you can go ahead and wrap up the interaction with whatever else you wanted to do. But if the 20% discount wasn't enough, you can then be guided through additional steps to try to retain the customer.

Obviously, you don't want to harass the customer or make them feel like they're not being listened to, but at the same time you want to make sure you have truly exhausted all techniques before putting the cancellation through. This is what NBA helps you do.

Before Einstein NBA existed, CSRs may have needed to make the decision on their own what benefits to offer people. This could mean they either provided too many or too steep discounts, leaving money on the table, or they didn't provide discounts to individuals they could have retained.

Can you imagine situations where Einstein NBA might be useful in a nonprofit capacity?

Einstein Prediction Builder

Einstein Prediction Builder is the primary focus of this section. Einstein Prediction Builder allows you to leverage the power of machine learning to make decisions. Unlike NBA, which directs the user to do something, Prediction Builder tells you the likelihood that something will happen so that you can act based on it.

Situations where I have seen Prediction Builder used effectively are as follows:

1. Fundraising departments need to calculate the likelihood a certain Opportunity will close.

2. Case managers want to know whether a client is likely to show up to an appointment.

3. Outreach staff want to know if someone will sign up for a program.

We go into the setup of Prediction Builder more in the next section, but for now it is important to understand that you give Prediction Builder the information about the kind of thing you are trying to predict (e.g., likelihood of enrolling in this program), and then you give it examples of clients who did enroll and did not enroll. Each of these situations provides information that will help you better allocate resources and assist clients.

After that, a machine learning algorithm looks at the data and determines the prediction. There's a lot of math involved in this, and we won't get too much into it, but those who know a bit about machine learning (or want to know more) can read on:

Salesforce uses the Linear Regression and Decision Tree algorithms for the prediction builder. It creates both, tests them, and chooses the one with the higher recall. It balances accuracy and precision. If you are using a yes/no (binary outcome), you can adjust the threshold in the Prediction Builder settings, which defaults to 50%.

Einstein Discovery (Tableau)

Einstein Discovery is a part of Salesforce that connects to Tableau. Tableau is a data visualization package that Salesforce acquired in 2019. Tableau does not require Salesforce to work, and in fact many people use Tableau with spreadsheets and other data to build interactive charts, graphs, and other data visualizations.

You can connect Tableau to Salesforce so that the source of the data that is on those charts and dashboards is your Salesforce data. This can allow you to create visualizations that Salesforce can't.

For example, I worked with a housing nonprofit that created heatmaps to see, by ZIP code, where their clients lived in the catchment area.

Salesforce can show a simple chart of client enrollments by ZIP code, but only when it was plotted in a heatmap did it become obvious that one corner of the catchment area with a large Hispanic population was underserved relative to the others. That allowed the organization to increase their targeted outreach with their bilingual staff to assist this population.

Tableau is very powerful all on its own as we have seen, and connecting it to Salesforce enables even further advantages. What of Einstein Discovery then? Einstein Discovery takes your Salesforce data into Tableau and shows you insights into it. This replaces or drastically reduces the time you need to spend coming up with insights. Instead, Discovery presents interesting patterns to you that it has detected in the data.

Einstein Discovery also enables you to do a variety of more complex analyses like Natural Language Processing (NLP) and go behind the machine learning algorithms to understand exactly how they came to their conclusion.

Einstein Bots

Einstein Bots are an extension of the chat bots that are used in Salesforce Service Cloud. Salesforce allows you to enable an Experience Cloud (community) with web chat so that you can talk directly to your clients.

For organizations that have a lot of interactions where people ask for the same information repeatedly, such as hours, programs available, or how to get started, you can extend the chat functionality with a chat bot.

A chat bot enables you to respond without human intervention to a variety of requests that you preprogram into the bot. If you've ever called a customer service line and been asked to say the department you want (e.g., Billing, Customer Service, or Technical Support), you've experienced something similar.

Einstein Bots go beyond the preprogrammed situation to leverage the power of Natural Language Processing (NLP). This means that no longer do you need to request that clients ask for something in a specific way. Instead, they can use their natural language to ask a question like "how do I join the program," and the NLP engine will understand that they are interested in intake and provide them with that information dynamically. This is true even when they haven't used the word "intake" or anything like it.

Salesforce provides a lot of documentation for Einstein, as seen in Figure 9-2.

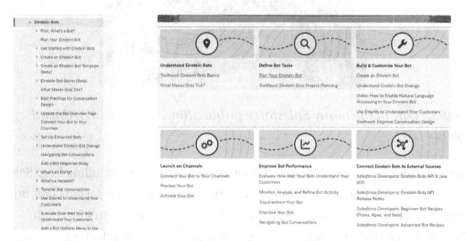

Figure 9-2. *A screenshot from the Salesforce website with Einstein Bots articles and Trailheads*

Ethics of Einstein

Before we continue and get into how to use Einstein Prediction Builder to improve your impact and outcomes, it's important that we talk about the ethics of AI. Salesforce has an Ethical AI Team whose role is to ensure that their Einstein products are not misused.

As a condition of using these tools, you also agree to follow certain requirements. If you don't, Salesforce will restrict your access to them to ensure that you don't discriminate against individuals or otherwise break the rules.

An example of a Salesforce publication about ethical AI is seen in Figure 9-3. You can see the full Acceptance Use policy at www.salesforce.com/content/dam/web/en_us/ www/documents/legal/Agreements/policies/ExternalFacing_Services_Policy.pdf.

Figure 9-3. *One of the many Salesforce publications on Ethical Artificial Intelligence (AI)*

Although there is more written about how to use AI ethically (including from Salesforce), the two main rules are that you cannot use as your predictors any protected class, and you cannot deny people service solely based on the Einstein Prediction Builder result.

What does that really mean? That means that when you are selecting the fields that you will feed into Einstein to make your prediction, you cannot use Gender, Race, Ethnicity, Disability Status, or any other protected class. The reason for this is that you don't want the model to use data like this to discriminate.

There are many stories of AIs that were designed improperly and ended up baking bias into them. For example, Apple used an AI tool to predict who should get promoted, based on who was successful in senior-level roles at Apple in the past. Unfortunately, the tool predicted that white males should be promoted, because those were the individuals who had ascended to senior roles in the past. The AI, trained on Apple employee data, had adopted the same bias as the humans at Apple.

For this reason, no protected class data can be used in Einstein Prediction Builder. Generally, your predictions aren't improved by knowing gender anyway, and there are other ways you can get the information that you need. For example, if you'd like to add Gender because you believe that women are more likely to miss appointments due to their unpredictable childcare, you can instead add as a predictor the number of children that a participant has or the number of minors/dependents they are responsible for.

The other thing that you must not do according to the Salesforce Ethical Use Agreement is make decisions on the sole basis of an Einstein Prediction Builder prediction. People are human, and many algorithms are black boxes. In Einstein's case, the most complex model that Einstein uses is called a Random Forest. This involves thousands of decision trees that are created and tested to see which one is most accurate. (Many Decision Trees make up the Random Forest.)

The result of this Random Forest model is a single decision tree that has been proven to be most accurate. This model is not a black box, because you can peer under the hood and see exactly which elements are responsible for each decision. On the other hand, there are models like the Artificial Neural Network (ANN) or the Support Vector Machine (SVM).

Although the Random Forest is a white box model as opposed to a black box like ANN/SVM, we still want to be careful that we are not making decisions for human beings solely based on the computerized model. Some basic reminders of probability are useful here: just because the chance of something happening is only 2% doesn't mean that if it happens, the model was wrong. Because with a 2% chance, in 100 repetitions of that event, it will most likely happen twice.

There are high-stakes examples of machine learning models unfairly penalizing individuals. One example is a probation and parole system developed by a third party that is used in Wisconsin, among other states. This model assigns individuals a recidivism risk based on criteria the company doesn't release, and the results can dictate the amount of supervision they are required to comply with.

Unfortunately, when the model over-assigns risk (as it has been accused of doing so by researchers and clinicians who do these kinds of analyses for a living), the individuals subjected to more invasive supervision are more likely to find themselves out of compliance and go back to prison, uprooting their lives again. Something as small as being late for a parole meeting because of a delay on public transit can throw someone's whole life into disarray.

For this reason, Salesforce will not permit you to use your predictions as the sole basis to deny someone services. Instead, the prediction must be one part of a holistic review of the client's situation that takes into account their situation. This prevents a biased algorithm or a client's individual situation from being penalized without the intervention of a trained case manager or other staff member.

Using Einstein Prediction Builder

Now that we've got that out of the way, it's time to dive into Einstein Prediction Builder itself. Every organization can create up to ten predictions for free, and one of those predictions can be active at a time. If you like Einstein Prediction Builder, you can buy a license and create as many predictions as you want.

There are six steps to using Einstein Prediction Builder. These six steps are also helpful if you want to attempt the Einstein Prediction Builder Accredited Professional (AP) exam, which I have held since 2021.

Define Your Use Case

First, you need to understand what you want to use Prediction Builder for. We've talked about a few of these examples. They include the likelihood someone will enroll, the amount you might receive for a donation, or whether someone will show up for an appointment.

You should spend time thinking about this use case and whether it supports your intended goals. It's cool to use machine learning, but you want to use it where it is a value-add and not just a cool bell and/or whistle.

Once you've identified your use case, you need to make sure that you have data that supports it, which is the focus of the next section.

Identify the Data That Supports Your Use Case

In order to predict something, you need to have data to base that prediction on. It's possible to ask Einstein Prediction Builder to predict anything based on any data, but that doesn't mean the prediction will be reliable. For example, you might ask Einstein to predict the amount of a donation (the Opportunity Amount) using the city, the time since the opportunity was created, and the day of the week it was last modified.

Einstein will go ahead and try to use that information to make the prediction, but because there's very little there that relates to the Opportunity amount, the prediction is likely to be of very poor quality.

The other thing you need to keep in mind here is that Einstein will look at the quality of the prediction (the R^2 for you stats nerds) to check the correlation of the prediction and the data it has. As we know, however, correlation does not equal causation. It's certainly possible for you to have two elements that happen to be correlated but are in fact not at all related. One example is in Figure 9-4, where the Divorce Rate in Maine matches up extremely closely with the per capita consumption of margarine.

Figure 9-4. *A spurious correlation from* `www.tylervigen.com/spurious-correlations`, *used with permission*

Obviously eating less margarine has zero impact on the divorce rate in that state, but the correlation makes it look like they are related. When we talk about having the domain knowledge, or the knowledge in your field to recognize when something is a true contributor to the outcome, this is what we mean.

Your experience in the area that you are trying to predict will help you determine if the program has face validity, which means that it appears to be a valid prediction based on what you know about people who receive that kind of support.

Once you've determined you have enough data to make a prediction and the prediction could be valid, you can go ahead to the next step where you make a prediction.

One more thing: all the data that you want to predict on must live on the same Object in Salesforce. If you want to predict using information from more than one object, you'll need to get that data from wherever it lives.

I have seen two approaches used effectively: if most of the data you need lives on one Object but some of it lives on another (e.g., Program Engagement has most of the fields with a couple of fields from Contact), you can use Formulas or Flows to populate that data on Program Engagement.

On the other hand, maybe the data you need is spread out over a whole bunch of objects. In that case, you can create a Custom Object called "Prediction" or something similar and have all the data flow to that object. Then you can tell Einstein to use the Prediction object.

Create Your Prediction

To create your prediction, you'll first need to go to the Setup Menu and Accept the Salesforce Ethical AI Terms. Once you've done that, you'll have a "Try Einstein" button that you can use to create your one free active prediction. Then you'll see the Get Started button, as shown in Figure 9-5.

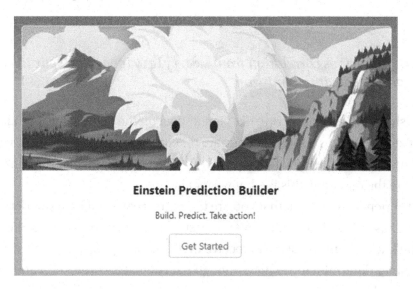

Figure 9-5. *The Einstein Get Started button*

The first thing Einstein wants to know, shown in Figure 9-6, is the name of your prediction. Give it something descriptive like "Propensity to Enroll," "Likelihood of Missing Appointment," or "Estimated Opportunity Value."

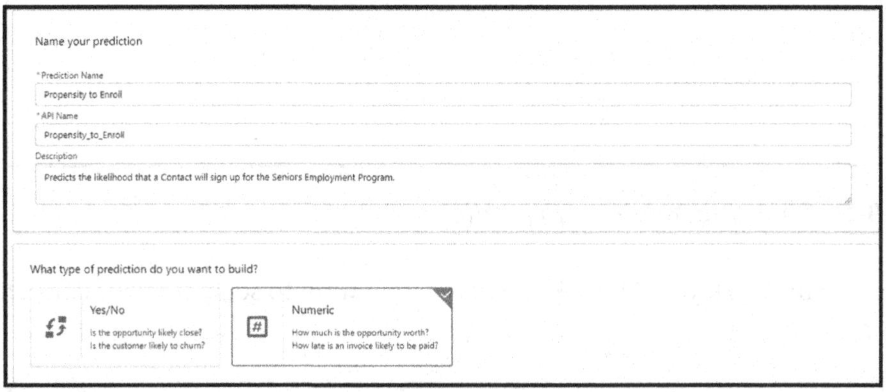

Figure 9-6. *Creating a prediction*

You'll be prompted to fill in an API name and a description. You also need to choose at this point if you'll be making a yes/no prediction or a numeric prediction. The reason that you're asked this early in the process is that Salesforce uses different algorithms for yes/no predictions (Logistic Regression) than they do for numeric predictions (Linear Regression and Random Forest.)

A numeric prediction is simply a yes/no. Will they miss their appointment? Yes or no. Will they enroll? Yes or no. On the other hand, a numeric prediction can be a currency amount (How much will they donate? $5,000) or a probability (How likely are they to enroll? 74%).

For this example, we'll assume that you're going to do a numeric prediction, but the steps are virtually identical either way.

Next, you'll be asked for the source Object of your prediction (Figure 9-7). Remember that we noted that all fields you want to feed into the prediction must live on the same object.

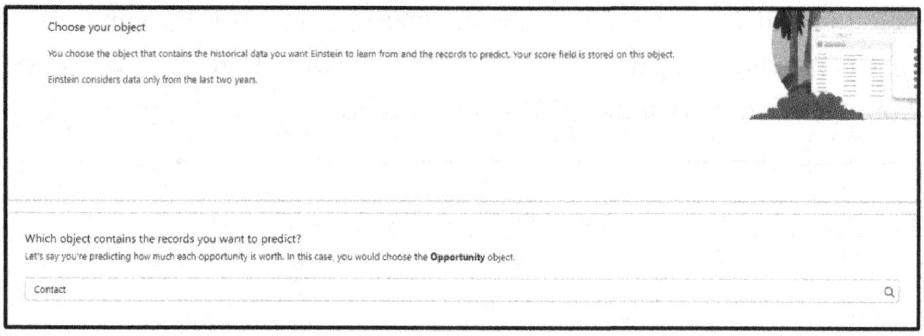

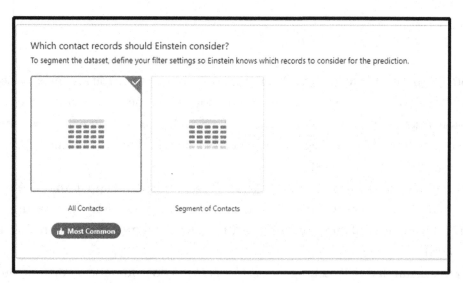

Figure 9-7. *Choosing an object to predict on*

After clicking Next, you'll be asked whether you want to segment your data, shown in Figure 9-8.

Figure 9-8. *Segmenting records*

Segmenting data is important because there may be situations where you are looking at the Contact or Account object and you want to limit the prediction to certain subsets, for example, only Organization Accounts or only Contacts living in a certain state.

Salesforce supports standard filters (equals, contains, greater than, last then, etc.) on basically any field on the chosen object to ensure that your data is segmented the way you want. If you'd like that prediction to apply to all Contacts, you can choose not to segment the data.

Next, you'll need to define the "yes" and "no" sets. This is shown in Figure 9-9. This can be a bit confusing. The "yes" set is the prediction set or the positive set. The thing that you are trying to predict occurred. The "yes" set doesn't have to be a good thing. The yes set on a prediction of "Will they miss their appointment" is those situations where they did miss their appointment.

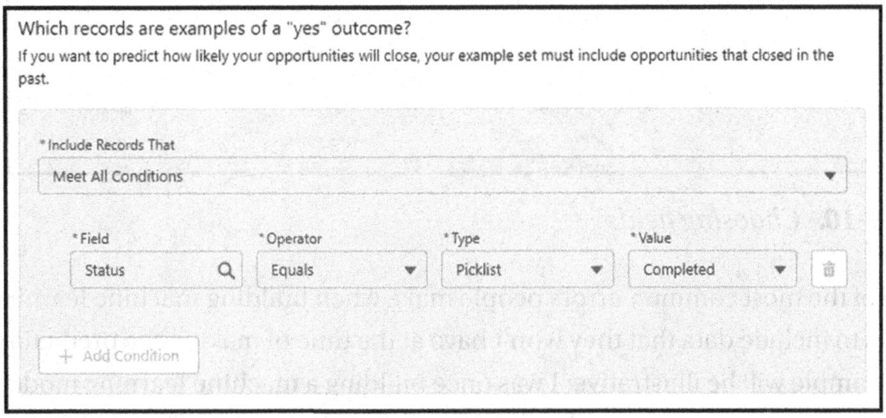

Figure 9-9. *Defining yes and no sets*

In contrast, the "no" set is those records where the thing you wanted to predict did not occur. The machine learning model uses this data to figure out what the differences are between the two sets to develop that prediction.

Like the previous step, you can also segment this data as needed. For example, you might define the "yes" set as people whose Service Delivery status equals "Missed" or "Unknown" in a situation where it's valuable to lump these two categories together.

After defining your yes and no sets, you'll need to choose which fields you'll be predicting on. This is shown in Figure 9-10. This is the data Salesforce will feed in to make the prediction. Generally, you'll use almost all of the fields on the object, but you need to handle this step carefully.

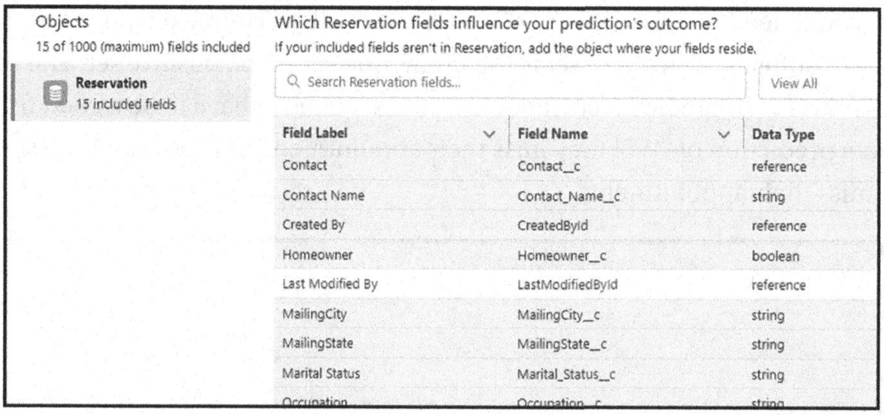

Figure 9-10. *Choosing fields*

One of the most common errors people make when building machine learning models is to include data that they won't have at the time of making the prediction.

An example will be illustrative: I was once building a machine learning model to predict whether a company would go bankrupt by analyzing their financial filings.

I made sure to exclude the Status column (which included "Going Concern" for organizations that were operating and "Bankrupt" for organizations that had gone bankrupt) but failed to exclude the column that reported whether the organization had filed for bankruptcy. This was a separate column in the dataset because some organizations that were still going concerns had filed for bankruptcy, but it wasn't finished yet.

What the machine learning model did was notice that any time an organization had "Filed for Bankruptcy" = Yes, it predicted that organization would go bankrupt. It completely ignored all the other data. Therefore, when tested on another sample of real companies, it was not able to predict their likelihood of going bankrupt because the new sample didn't have that column filled in.

Another example, more relevant to nonprofits: if you are predicting whether someone will show up for an appointment by looking at their Service Delivery data, you can't include any columns that the case manager would fill out after the service delivery happened, like the client's progress toward goals, their mood, or whatever notes the case manager might fill in. These might mislead the model into making conclusions based on data that won't exist for an appointment that hasn't happened yet.

So, be careful when you select the fields you'll use to make your prediction. Don't be afraid to include fields you don't think will be relevant, but ensure you exclude any that won't exist when your prediction is being made in the real world.

Review, Iterate, and Enable Your Prediction

This is the last step before you review your prediction. Salesforce will make a quick estimate of how effective it thinks your prediction will be. If the prediction is between 60% and 95%, you're golden. This will be a useful prediction.

If the accuracy is below 60%, it's closer to a coin flip (or potentially even worse than chance!) and therefore probably not useful. If it's above 95%, counterintuitively, this is probably not a good prediction either. The reason for this is that in the real world, models are rarely this accurate. If yours is, it's likely because you've included some datapoint that is influencing the model in a way that it's not really analyzing what you want it to be analyzing. An example prediction scorecard is shown in Figure 9-11.

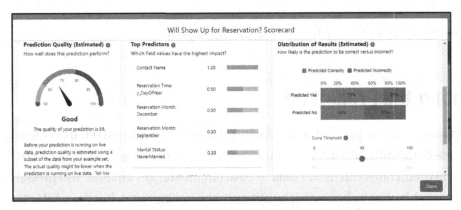

Figure 9-11. *Prediction scorecard*

If you need to make tweaks, now's the time. You can go back and adjust the fields, change the segmentation, or make any other changes you need to improve the prediction estimate. Note that this is an estimate. Salesforce won't know how your data performs in the real world for a while.

One nice aspect of this Scorecard is that you can see what fields are most predictive of the outcome. This can help you explain the prediction to other people.

Monitor Your Prediction

Once you are satisfied and you click Submit, Einstein begins churning away on the model. It can take over 24 hours for Einstein to work its magic and produce an updated Scorecard. Once it tells you that a scorecard is available, you can review it to ensure that all looks sound, and you are ready to proceed.

You can activate your prediction and then it can be used, as described next.

Deploy and Use Your Prediction

Once you've activated your prediction, you need to put it somewhere. Because Einstein created a special field to store the data from your prediction, you can put that on a Page Layout, use it in List View, and embed it into a report or anywhere else you might find yourself using a field in Salesforce.

You can also use a formula field to bring the prediction onto a related object. Figure 9-12 shows a prediction field on a list view.

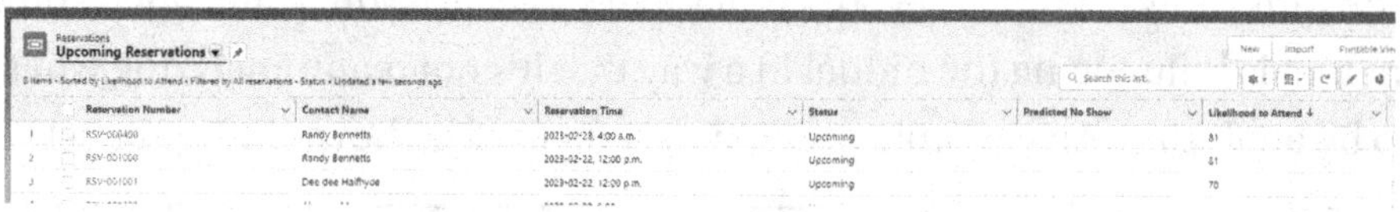

Figure 9-12.   *A list view with a prediction field on it*

Updating the Prediction

Einstein will tweak the prediction internally over time to ensure that it uses the most up-to-date data. Initially it will use all the data that it has access to, but over time it will refresh the prediction with newer data in case circumstances change. You probably won't notice this change because it happens in the background, but the goal is to ensure that your predictions are as efficient as they can be.

Collecting Survey Data via Experience Cloud

One of the ways that you can get data into Salesforce is using a Salesforce Experience Cloud. Experience Cloud used to be called Community Cloud, and you'll find many people still refer to the website that is created as a Community for this reason. The certification was also called Certified Community Cloud Consultant until very recently.

Whether you call it an Experience Cloud, a Community, a Community Cloud, or a Site, what it represents is the ability to get data into Salesforce from an external website that you can give your clients or other stakeholders access to. No longer do they need to fill out surveys that you then manually enter into the back end. You can now expose pages, Flows, objects, and other Salesforce data directly to clients.

Now, it's important that you understand that there is a licensing and fee consideration to keep in mind when building an Experience Cloud site. An unauthenticated experience is like a guest or kiosk experience. You can show your client information, and they can put information onto the website, but they can't get anything back out. This is the most common situation you'll likely experience when you fill out a Contact Us form or otherwise interact with a website online.

Figure 9-13 shows a survey on an unauthenticated experience.

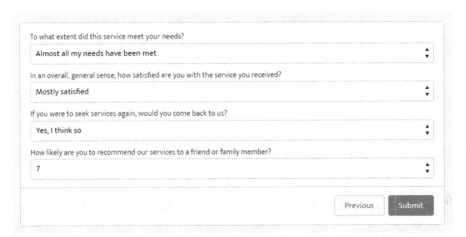

Figure 9-13. *An unauthenticated survey form*

The other kind of experience is an authenticated Experience. This involves creating an account that you can log in to. This allows more advanced connections between your data inside Salesforce and what you're doing inside the Experience Cloud. It also takes licenses, and licenses cost money.

For this chapter, we'll assume that you are creating an unauthenticated Experience. This can be done in a Sandbox or Production environment. Like authenticated Experiences, Unauthenticated Experiences can show data, run Flows, and allow you to submit information that goes into Salesforce. They lack the Client ID of an authenticated user, however, so you can't pull unique data out of the system that differs based on who is looking at it.

The first step to creating an Experience Cloud is to navigate to the Setup Menu. From the setup search, type Digital Experiences and choose "All Sites" from the submenu, as shown in Figure 9-14. This has been the source of some frustration for users and Salesforce admin staff alike as this used to be called something else.

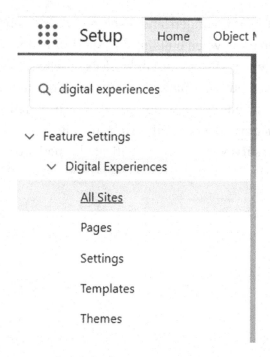

Figure 9-14. *Navigating to the Salesforce Experience Cloud setup*

Some organizations might need to enable Digital Experiences, as shown in Figure 9-15. You can go ahead and check the box to do so. Note that once you enable Digital Experiences, you cannot disable it; however, if you never use the functionality, it doesn't affect your org in any way.

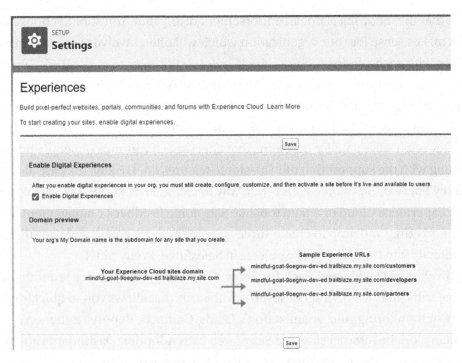

Figure 9-15. *Enabling Digital Experiences in a sandbox*

Once Digital Experiences are enabled and you've navigated to All Sites, you can create your Experience Cloud. For more detailed information on creating and working with Experience Clouds, see *Practical Guide to Salesforce Experience Clouds* by Philip Weinmeister (2022), published by Apress.

Leveraging AppExchange Solutions to Better Model Outcomes

Did you know that Salesforce has an app store? If you've used Salesforce for a while, you've probably come across an AppExchange solution or been recommended to check one out. When you want to integrate Salesforce with a variety of other tools like DocuSign, FormStack, or Qualtrics, there is an AppExchange solution involved.

There are some impact measurement tools you can check out in the AppExchange to better model your outcomes. Although a homegrown solution is strongly preferred, sometimes the AppExchange allows you to speed up the process and get ready quicker.

Note that the following is not an endorsement of any tool. You should choose the tool that makes sense for your organization which will often involve some research and discussion with each vendor.

Salesforce Labs produces a variety of tools that are useful for impact measurement and outcome evaluation. Salesforce Labs is the home for products produced by Salesforce employees that are not officially in the roadmap for the full product. This means they often solve smaller problems that affect specific groups of people but don't come along with the support that full Salesforce features do. Luckily, they are also free!

Survey Force by Salesforce Labs is one way to create surveys quicker and easier than using an Experience Cloud or a paid tool like Salesforce Feedback Management. It allows you to quickly drag and drop to create surveys, send them via email, and capture the results directly into Contact or Case objects in Salesforce. Pretty nifty!

AppExchange Dashboard Pack for Sales, Marketing, and Service is another useful Salesforce Labs product. It's a set of seven dashboards that allows you to quickly get started with monitoring your organization's Leads, Contacts, Reports, and more.

Similarly, on the internal side, the Salesforce Labs Adoption Dashboards are handy. They allow you to understand who is using your Salesforce organization.

Salesforce, in cooperation with the Climate Justice Lab, has also produced a tool called the **Grants Content Kit**. This is a very interesting tool that allows you to store the information used to apply for grants right inside Salesforce. When you go to apply for a new grant, you can mix and match the different content items to build a new grant application much quicker than you did before.

One way that this tool can be utilized effectively is by writing up grant content that focuses on the impact you've recorded from the other tools that you've used throughout this book. When you find yourself applying for a grant, you have a ready-made source of impact information that you can rely on to tell your story more effectively and to increase the likelihood that you are selected for that funding.

Although the Grants Content Kit was designed specifically for climate change organizations, the data model is flexible and applies equally well to a variety of organizations. From the Grants Content Kit documentation, you can find examples of sections that you can create in the tool to quickly add these into your grant application narratives. These include the following:

- Program narrative

- Executive summary

- Statement of need

- Project objectives

- Plan of action

- Goals and objectives

- Budget narrative

Conclusion

There are a variety of ways to extend Salesforce using AppExchange solutions and add-ons like Einstein. You should explore whether any of these are right for your organization and integrate them if they are.

CHAPTER 10

Conclusion

We find ourselves at the end of this journey. Hopefully, you have come away with a better understanding of impact measurement and outcome evaluation and how you may apply these principles to the work that you do every day. The rest of this chapter is focused on where you go from here.

Becoming more data-driven is not something that happens overnight. It takes a dedicated effort from the top of the organization on down to ensure that you are collecting the kind of information that you need and using it to guide your organization's decisions.

The Future of Salesforce and Program Evaluation

As of this writing, Salesforce has recently rolled out Nonprofit Cloud or NPC. This represents the biggest change in the Salesforce Nonprofit ecosystem perhaps in Salesforce's history. Instead of Nonprofit Cloud Case Management (NCCM) being built on top of Salesforce with Lightning Web Components (LWC) used for specific functionality, NPC uses the OmniStudio/Vlocity technologies that Salesforce acquired in 2020.

Gone are the Service Delivery and Program Engagement objects. In their place, you'll find Program Enrollment and Benefit. NCCM formerly used the Household Account model where each participant in your program is a Contact that is attached to an Account that represents their Household.

In NPC, they have moved to the Person Account model. This model combines elements of the Contact and Account objects into Salesforce in one. Other objects that are new in NPC include the Care Plan (replacing the Case Plan), Benefit Type and Benefit Assignment, and the Referral object. Many of these changes represent a return to the way that other organizations had done things pre-NCCM. For example, many organizations call someone joining a program an enrollment, and only in NCCM did

© Dustin MacDonald 2023
D. MacDonald, *Impact Measurement and Outcomes Evaluation Using Salesforce for Nonprofits*,
https://doi.org/10.1007/978-1-4842-9708-7_10

they change that to "engagement." It has once again returned to program engagement. Similarly, the Case object in NCCM is used for referrals; however, in the new NPC, you now have access to a dedicated Referral object.

Some of these changes should make adopting NPC easier for organizations that are new to Salesforce. Given that so much of the work of impact measurement and outcome evaluation is "platform agnostic," you should not worry that these changes will make it difficult for you to apply the principles of this book.

Salesforce has also written about impact measurement, and this is an interest of Salesforce. It is possible that in the future, Salesforce rolls out a dedicated impact measurement tool. If so, rest assured that the principles you've learned here will still apply.

Next Steps in Your Learning

There are numerous options for improving your knowledge and skills in this area. These include certifications, Trailmixes, and more formal programs like degrees. Continuous learning is an important part of the work of every nonprofit professional, and a mix of Salesforce and non-Salesforce learning is recommended to keep your skills sharp and avoid the myopia that can sometimes happen when you restrict yourself to a single technology platform's ecosystem.

If you don't already have professional development time "baked in" to your weekly schedule, it's highly recommended. Scott D. Miller, who is the founder of the International Center for Clinical Excellence, has done a lot of work on deliberate practice and what the best performing therapists do differently. His research has found that the highest performing therapists make 7 hours a week to focus on improving their skills, while the lowest performing therapists spend just 30 minutes.

Such is the case in nonprofit leadership, requirements gathering, Salesforce configuration, or impact measurement: the best ones continue to build their skills.

Salesforce Certifications and Accredited Professionals

Salesforce Certified Nonprofit Cloud Consultant

The Salesforce Certified Nonprofit Cloud Consultant (see Figure 10-1) is an excellent credential for those who are interested in learning more about NCCM and NPSP. This exam covers the whole Nonprofit Cloud and allows you to demonstrate that you understand how to assess potential solutions and choose the best option.

Figure 10-1. *My Nonprofit Cloud Consultant certification*

Salesforce includes a Trailmix that is approximately 35 hours of learning to prepare for this certification. The exam guide recommends that you have approximately 2-5 years of nonprofit experience. This is because the exam assumes a fair amount of "domain knowledge" that is not specifically tested but covers more general aspects of nonprofits and especially fundraising. NPSP is very heavily represented in this exam and is outside the scope of this book.

Note that as of this writing, the Nonprofit Consultant exam has not been updated to reflect the new Nonprofit Cloud (NPC) and probably will not be for quite some time. For this reason, if you have a choice between learning NCCM/NPSP and the new NPC and wish to earn the certification, you should focus on NCCM/NPSP first.

Salesforce Certified OmniStudio Consultant

With the change to OmniStudio coming as part of the NPC rollout, Salesforce Certified OmniStudio Consultant (see Figure 10-2) is another excellent option for a certification. This certification is an excellent introduction to the world of OmniStudio including FlexCards, OmniScripts, Data Raptors, Integration Procedures, and some of the other tools that are based on them.

Figure 10-2. *My OmniStudio Consultant certification*

FlexCards display relevant information about a Contact or other record that you're looking at. These are custom-built Lightning Web Components (LWC), but they don't require any coding. In addition to displaying information about the record, you can also add buttons that allow you to act on the information or to take other actions.

Data Raptors, despite the name, have nothing to do with dinosaurs. Instead, Data Raptors allow you to take in information from Salesforce. Once you've loaded it in, you can manipulate or transform it and then save it back to Salesforce. This allows you to do complex manipulations that would not be possible otherwise.

In the past, if you wanted to do a complex ETL (Extract, Transform, and Load) operation like this, you would require a middleware tool like MuleSoft or a developer to custom code something for you. Instead, with Data Raptors, you can do this from a point and click interface with a bit of JSON (JavaScript Object Notation) to ensure you've mapped things correctly.

Integration Procedures (IP) are like Data Raptors, but they allow you to pull information from both Salesforce and third parties. They take the difficulty of interacting with an Application Programming Interface (API) and make it much simpler. Like Salesforce Flows, you use a visual interface with "blocks" to set up how the IP will work.

OmniScripts are very similar to Salesforce Flow, but they are much more powerful. OmniScripts allow you to proceed through guided flows to display information, take actions, collect data, and other similar items. The major advantage of an OmniScript is that they can take advantage of Data Raptors and Integration Procedures to pull information in from external sources in a way that Flows would require Apex to do.

There are some other OmniStudio components covered in the exam. These include the Business Rules Engine (BRE) and the Decision Explainer. The Business Rules Engine allows you to perform calculations and make decisions by programming the logic into the system in advance. If you wanted to do this with NCCM, you would have needed either a very complex Flow or Apex coding.

With the BRE, you can include all the logic inside your OmniScript. When a client is interested in receiving services from a nonprofit, for example, your OmniScript can collect eligibility information and determine not just whether they are eligible, but how much of a benefit they can receive. This can work even for complex calculations like business tax owed, Low Income Home Energy Assistance Program (LIHEAP) benefit amounts, or emergency pandemic assistance payments.

This exam is very high level, in contrast to the Certified OmniStudio Developer credential. If you understand the purpose of each of the features and functionality, you will be well-prepared to take the exam.

Salesforce also provides a Trailmix which will help prepare you for the OmniStudio exam. As of this writing, you can access it at `https://trailhead.salesforce.com/users/strailhead/trailmixes/prepare-for-your-salesforce-omni-studio-consultant-credential`.

Einstein Prediction Builder Accredited Professional

Einstein Prediction Builder was covered extensively in Chapter 8. If you are working at a Salesforce Partner, also called a System Integrator (SI) by Salesforce themselves, you have access to a second type of certification. These certifications are called Salesforce Accredited Professional (AP).

Salesforce provides their partners with a learning management system (LMS) called Partner Learning Camp. On the Partner Learning Camp, you can access courses for a variety of Salesforce tools and platforms, to help you prepare for exams.

One of these courses is a comprehensive overview of how to use Einstein Prediction Builder. It also functions as preparation for the Einstein Prediction Builder Accredited Professional exam, which reviews things like how to set up Einstein Prediction Builder, how to avoid leaky fields, how to interpret the prediction scorecard, and other items that are important in effective use of the tool.

See Figure 10-3 for my Einstein Accredited Professional badge, issued via the Credly platform.

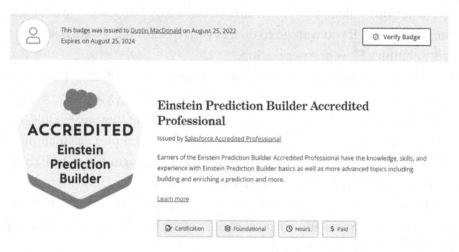

Figure 10-3. *An Accredited Professional badge*

Salesforce also provides access to the Einstein Next Best Action (NBA) Accredited Professional if you are interested in earning this credential.

Net Zero Cloud Accredited Professional

Net Zero Cloud is one of Salesforce's newest offerings. It is a complex data model and takes a lot to learn, but it is valuable. Net Zero refers to the concept of having zero carbon emissions.

Achieving net zero emissions means that all the carbon emissions that an organization releases are recorded. Then through the purchase of carbon offsets, direct air capture and storage (DACS), or other methods, an equivalent amount of the carbon released is removed from the atmosphere.

Achieving net zero carbon emissions is an important goal in the fight against climate change. This can also be an excellent goal for a nonprofit that wants to demonstrate their commitment to climate justice.

The role of the M&E specialist in the Net Zero process cannot be overstated, and the tools in this book can also be applied to achieving Net Zero and the benefits that it provides. For example, one study estimated that the value of a ton of carbon removed from the atmosphere was a little under $30.[1] This can be a major contributor to your social return on investment (SROI) ratio, as the cost of a carbon offset credit can be found under a dollar per ton.

Net Zero Cloud allows you to track Scope 1, Scope 2, and Scope 3 emissions. Scope 1 emissions are those that are directly under the control of the organization and are direct emissions such as driving a car or burning fuel to operate a generator.

Scope 2 emissions are those that a company uses indirectly when they purchase energy. For example, if you live in an area where energy is produced by a coal-fired power plant, you are indirectly responsible for Scope 2 emissions based on the amount of power you use.

Scope 3 emissions are those where you didn't produce the emissions at all but rather purchased something from someone who did produce emissions. These are the hardest to track and often represent the bulk of the emissions that an organization is responsible for. For example, if you purchase a set of truck tires from a manufacturer, they likely used fossil fuels to produce them and therefore have emitted greenhouse gases.

Earning the Net Zero Cloud Accredited Professional (AP) exam will help you demonstrate your commitment to preventing climate change and can open new avenues for your organization in advocacy, awareness, and impact.

Trailmixes

Salesforce's learning platform called Trailhead is an excellent resource for learning about the platform. There are thousands of badges, modules, Superbadges, and reading materials accessible on all areas of the platform and in related topics such as user experience (UX) design, corporate social responsibility (CSR), and even management.

The Salesforce Impact Measurement Trailmix is an excellent resource for reinforcing the learning from this book. You can access it at `https://trailhead.salesforce.com/users/sfdo/trailmixes/impact-measurement`.

---

[1] `http://livebettermagazine.com/article/hdr-sroi-how-to-measure-green/`

The Impact Measurement Trailmix includes components on the basics of impact measurement, how to develop a strategic plan, how to create a theory of change, how to data modeling, how to measure your outcomes, and other elements you'll be very familiar with.

Another Trailhead you might find valuable is the Tactics for Impact Management Trailhead accessible at `https://trailhead.salesforce.com/content/learn/modules/tactics-for-impact-management`.

This Trailmix contains modules on how to integrate impact measurement into your core strategy and how to ensure that the decisions you make are based on the evidence you have collected, a reminder to pursue continuous improvement and evidence-building, and more. This is a great companion to the Impact Measurement Trailmix discussed earlier.

While both Trailmixes were created by Salesforce themselves, there are other Trailmixes created by community members that you may find interesting. A few of them are linked as follows:

1. SFDC Values & Impact Mix by Sara Haque (`https://trailhead.salesforce.com/users/shaque/trailmixes/values-impact-trailmix-sfdc`)

2. Impact + Salesforce by Honour McDaniel (`https://trailhead.salesforce.com/users/impactamerica/trailmixes/impact-salesforce`)

3. Green Impact Salesforce 101 by Dan Connors (`https://trailhead.salesforce.com/users/dconnors4/trailmixes/green-impact-salesforce-101`)

You may find that putting together a Trailmix yourself helps give your employees the background they need in reporting or impact measurement, so they can understand the context that your changes are occurring in. This can help them better appreciate the changes and ensure they take them on. To learn more about how to use a change management process, see Chapter 7.

Degrees and Certificates

Universities are currently facing a lot of criticism for increasing tuition that has made it harder for people to earn degrees. One source puts the increase in college costs at 1200% since 1980, while the Consumer Price Index (CPI) that represents the average increase in costs has risen about 236%.[2]

Despite the increased cost, most nonprofit employees hold a degree. There are a variety of options for an M&E professional who wants to earn a degree inexpensively. If you don't hold a bachelor's degree, an online option like Western Governor's University (WGU) is an inexpensive option.

WGU's tuition for undergraduates is $4500 per 6-month term. You take one course at a time, starting with a pre-course knowledge exam. If you score high enough on the pretest to indicate you already have the knowledge that the course provides, you can simply skip to the final exam. A passing grade on the final exam means you've earned that credit.

WGU offers degrees in Business Administration, Information Technology, Finance, and Accounting – all of which would be excellent for a nonprofit professional.

It is technically possible to earn a degree in as short as 6 months, though most people take closer to 2 years to earn their Bachelor's. At $4,500 per 6-month term, a 2-year completion time would cost just under $18,000. WGU, like all the universities discussed in this section, provides financial aid including grants and scholarships alongside loans accessed by completing the Free Application for Federal Student Aid (FAFSA).

If you already hold a bachelor's degree and are interested in a master's degree, your options widen significantly. You may choose to pursue a Master of Public Administration (MPA), a Master of Arts in Nonprofit Management, or even a Master of Business Administration (MBA).

Several inexpensive programs exist in each of these areas. For a cheap MPA, you can investigate the Southern Arkansas University whose MPA as of this writing is just $10,548 for in-state students or $16,524 for out-of-state students.

To pursue a Nonprofit Management program, you could consider the Master of Arts in Philanthropy and Nonprofit Development at the University of Northern Iowa which clocks in at $16,170 for both in-state and out-of-state students this year.

---

[2] www.visualcapitalist.com/rising-cost-of-college-in-u-s/

For an inexpensive MBA, you could look to Eastern University, whose Master of Business Administration in Organizational Management has just become available with a price tag of $9,900. (Full disclosure: I am a graduate of Eastern University, though I did not take the MBA program.)

For those who already hold a degree, there are many inexpensive certificates available out there as well. The big takeaway is that education does not need to break the bank. Many online programs exist that are designed to be taken part-time by individuals who are working so that you can continue to build your skills. I have earned all but my first qualification (a diploma equivalent to an American associate degree) online.

How to Implement What You've Learned in Your Organization

It's all well and good to learn something new, but translating that into *praxis* or action is another idea entirely. The concept of knowledge fade and the forgetting curve applies here: most of the information that you learn will be forgotten. Estimates are as high as 80% of the information that you learn will be forgotten within 30 days if you do not regularly reinforce it.

This means that your goals are twofold: first, to ensure you don't forget the information contained in this book and, second, to be able to apply that knowledge across the organization. The higher up in the organization you find yourself, the easier applying this information will be. At the same time, there exists the possibility to apply impact measurement and outcome evaluation even as a frontline employee.

Remembering What You Learned

Read and reread: Returning to the concept of the knowledge fade, you may find yourself needing to read something several times before it really sinks in. Rereading the content in this book can help ensure that you remember those pieces that you had forgotten previously and can help ensure that you continue to apply these lessons.

Practice the basics: Scott D. Miller's deliberate practice comes into place here. Ensuring that you make time every week to practice the basics of impact measurement and outcome evaluation will keep it fresh in your mind. This doesn't have to be anything as involved as a full degree program but can be as simple as ensuring you read an article each week or you look at a program or service you offer and examine whether there are ways to make the delivery more intentional and make the evaluation more data-driven.

Write it down: You remember something more effectively when you use more parts of your brain to consume the information. Reading is one way to stimulate your brain. So is writing it down. Some studies even support the idea that writing on physical paper engages your brain more fully than taking digital notes. Finally, practicing what you've learned helps solidify that knowledge.

Establish a Center of Excellence: A Center of Excellence is a team in an organization whose role is to provide best practices, leadership, and guidance to others in the organization. Consider forming a Center of Excellence at your organization to be a resource to all who are interested in utilizing data-driven approaches in their work.

A Center of Excellence can be as simple as one or two people who are designated as the "data people" but can be more formal than that and represent a team who has the responsibility to produce templates, guides, and recommended approaches for ensuring that the principles of good impact measurement and outcomes are followed throughout the organization.

Putting It into Practice

Establish an action plan: Decide how you want to incorporate impact measurement and outcome evaluation into your day-to-day, and make an action plan with goals for how to get there. If you're uncertain of where to begin, consider asking your supervisor what would make their life easier.

This idea of "managing up" can both give you awareness of the goals you would need to meet when you get promoted and help build buy-in for your new efforts.

Find sponsors: In the chapter on change management (Chapter 7), we discussed the importance of a change management sponsor. Your organization should ideally have a measurement and evaluation sponsor. While that may be yourself if you are the M&E specialist, you should aim to involve senior leadership in this effort as well.

As a director you may report to a C-level individual like the chief strategy officer and should aim to get them onboard as well. A data-driven approach works best when everyone is moving in the same direction.

Seek out small projects: You don't need to do anything grand to get started. Simply evaluating your organization's data model and beginning to clean things up can help you build momentum.

Starting to become more data-driven is a win to celebrate, and you don't need to start with any grand projects. As you gain more experience and success making changes in the organization, you will find it easier and easier, and larger projects will present themselves and be attainable.

Conclusion

Building effective, data-driven organizations is a marathon, not a sprint. You've taken the first steps into getting there. I celebrate and congratulate you and look forward to hearing that your organization's ability to serve your clients has been improved through this work.

As you move toward a data-driven organization, there will be fits and starts. There will be initiatives that work, and others that fall short. This is okay and is part of the learning process. As you become more strategic, and your institutional knowledge builds, this will occur less and less, but you will get there.

As they say, do not let the perfect be the enemy of the good. Good luck, and happy learning!

Index

Printed in the United States
by Baker & Taylor Publisher Services